The Accent Handbook

A Practical Guide to Learning Accents

Jessica Hammett and Lottie Williams-Burrell

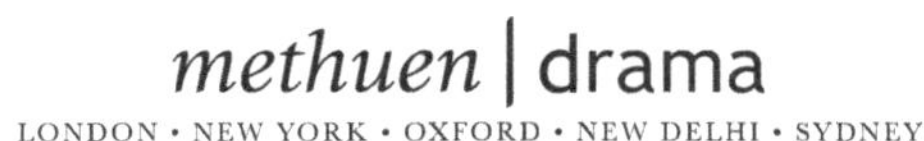

METHUEN DRAMA
Bloomsbury Publishing Plc
50 Bedford Square, London, WC1B 3DP, UK
1385 Broadway, New York, NY 10018, USA
29 Earlsfort Terrace, Dublin 2, Ireland

BLOOMSBURY, METHUEN DRAMA and the Methuen Drama logo are trademarks of
Bloomsbury Publishing Plc

First published in Great Britain 2024

A catalogue record for this book is available from the British Library.

ISBN: HB: 978-1-3502-4332-3
PB: 978-1-3502-4333-0
ePDF: 978-1-3502-4334-7
eBook: 978-1-3502-4335-4

Typeset by Deanta Global Publishing Services, Chennai, India
Printed and bound in Great Britain

To find out more about our authors and books visit www.bloomsbury.com
and sign up for our newsletters.

The Accent Handbook

Jess

*To my parents Sarah and Stephen Hammett,
whose voices will always remain with me.*

Lottie

*To my wonderful family, with a special dedication to Mum for your unwavering
support and encouragement, to Dad for watching over and being so vivid in times
of need and to my great loves, Tom and Lyra.*

Contents

List of figures

List of exercises

Acknowledgements

We are grateful to many for their help in producing this book.

To our colleagues at Mountview, in particular Sally Ann Gritton for her support. To our contributors, Dr Tom Campion for the generous donation of medical images, Sandy McInnes for his wonderful illustrations, Alistair Hobson for his audio editing prowess (and patience!) and Jude McSpadden of Phonimation for her beautiful tongue animations. To everyone who provided an accent recording, we are incredibly grateful.

We are indebted to the coaches at The Dialect Agency headed by the incomparable Jill McCullough for their expertise, critical readings and, most importantly, their fellowship. Thank you to Sonja Field, Jacob Hajjar, Sam Lilja, Sarah McGuinness, Helen Simmons, Naomi Todd and Anne Whitaker.

To Dudley Knight, Phil Thompson, Andrea Caban, Julie Foh, Tyler Seiple, Nathan Crocker and the entire Knight-Thompson Speechwork community. Your work has been transformative and has inspired several exercises in this book.

To Alex Christofi for his advice in producing an actual, real-life book! To all our test readers for their time and valuable feedback: Eva Feiler, Chris Lakewood, Andrea Lewis, Henry Lloyd-Hughes, David Jarzen, Kate Malyon, Marco Morbidelli, Alan Pearson and Sam Woolf.

Lastly, thank you to our students and clients, past and present. We continue to be inspired by you and offer this book as a handy friend to be by your side throughout your professional lives.

Jess: To my brother Leo Hammett, and dear friends Sophie Tilbury, Frances and Laura Pattison, Janine Catalano, Sandy McInnes, Alice Lacey and Chris Griffin for their unending love and encouragement. And to Stewart and Catriona Coltart for the frequent use of their shepherd's hut!

Lottie: To Sally Ann Gritton for her guidance and wisdom, Sterre Maier, Andrea Lewis, Alan Pearson and Marco Morbidelli for the camaraderie, conversations and cake, and the Mountview Performance team for their professional support and friendship. And to my maternity tribe for rallying round when I needed to edit and for cheering me over the finish line.

Introduction

There is no such thing as an ugly accent, like there's no such thing as an ugly flower.

– David Crystal

What is an accent?

Every human being with the power of speech has an accent. Accent is, quite simply, the way we **sound** when we speak; the way we **pronounce** words and string them together.

Accent vs dialect

The words 'accent' and 'dialect' are often used interchangeably but they mean slightly different things.

The word 'dialect' usually refers to a way of speaking which includes its own **vocabulary** and forms of **grammar**. Someone who says, 'I ain't seen the lift' is using a different dialect to one who says, 'I haven't seen the elevator'. Dialect (grammar and word choice) is often in the hands of the writer.

This book focuses on **accent**. This refers to **pronunciation**. For example, some speakers of English will pronounce the following pairs of words the same, and others will pronounce them differently:

'look' and 'luck'
'oil' and 'aisle'
'reap' and 'rip'
'pause' and 'pours'

And let's not get into the different ways 'sheet' can be said!

What are accents composed of?

Accents are a mix of:

Shapes: the way speech muscles move and position themselves to 'shape' the accent

Patterns: rhythm, stress and pitch patterns

Sounds: vowels and consonants, like 'EE' and 'OO' or 'T' and 'M'

When people use very similar shapes, sounds and patterns to speak, they are often thought of as having the same accent. It's worth noting, though, that accents vary between individuals within communities and groups. Learning accents for performance involves:

- noticing the **shapes**, **patterns** and **sounds**
- copying and remembering them
- making them your own, so they feel and sound as if you use them everyday

How you notice, copy, remember and reproduce the accent for performance depends on you, and this book offers a variety of ways to do it.

Accent and identity

The second we open our mouths to speak we share a portion of our identity. Beyond the actual words we choose our accents communicate a lot about us, whether we realize it or not.

Do you speak in the same way as your immediate family or those you shared a home with growing up? What about your friends or colleagues? The way we humans speak reflects our life experiences, starting from the moment we're born.

At the same time, accents and dialects aren't fixed in individuals or communities. They shift and reshape. Rather than having strict 'rules', they have 'tendencies'. Why? Well, why do we humans speak at all? According to need. The need to communicate; to share information, to be heard and understood by others.

People shift between different modes of speaking based on what will work best for them at that moment. These shifts often happen unconsciously. Someone might sound different when they're trying to make their friends laugh, compared to when they talk to their boss. Moving to a new city can alter someone's accent, as can a change in social group.

Accent is more than just geography

There is so much more to accents than where we're born. The way we speak can also be influenced by our:

- environment
- age
- gender

- sexuality
- occupation
- ethnicity
- socioeconomic background
- education
- who we are speaking to
- where we are speaking

Accents can also change over **time**, either within an individual person, within a geographical area or culturally within a group. A study in 2000 found that Queen Elizabeth II's accent had changed between the 1950s and 1980s. They concluded that her speech had been influenced by and reflected the changes in society over the years.[1]

Accent bias

Whether we like it or not, and whether we're aware of it or not, everyone has biases regarding accents. All over the world, different forms of speech are given more or less value than others. Some accents have been and continue to be held in high regard by various communities. Other accents, and the communities they're identified with, are involved in a seemingly endless cycle of marginalization, stereotyping, prejudice and discrimination.

An actor's own accent biases may make some accents less appealing to learn. It's crucial to acknowledge and work through these biases. Unchecked biases could prevent an actor from authentically inhabiting an accent and therefore, the character. The true value of an accent for the actor is its ability to fulfil the expressive needs of the character, illuminate the world the character inhabits and help tell the story.

Why this book?

Perhaps you need to learn a specific accent quickly for an audition. Or maybe you got the part but want to work on the details. Maybe you're struggling with a sound or feature of the accent and can't seem to crack it. Perhaps you're looking for a way to bring accent and character together.

Whatever it is, we can offer solutions. This handbook has been designed with the needs and aims of the actor in mind. You'll find practical approaches to doing accents and a selection of accent recordings. You can learn directly from these recordings or use your own accent samples.

We don't believe there is a 'one size fits all' method for learning an accent. People learn in different ways. Some of us need to **see** or **read** something to understand it, some need to **hear** it, while others need to physically **feel** and **experience** it. Many of us need to do a combination of the above. Finding the right process for you is key.

Different accents may require different approaches or 'ways in'. Sometimes, the underlying **rhythm** jumps out straight away. Sometimes, a particular **consonant** sound provides the 'hook'. Even thinking of a shape or direction can be key. We'll help you capitalize on whatever connects you to a particular accent.

This book:

- contains accent recordings and guides for listening
- will help you make sense of accent features
- offers varied opportunities to practise with easy-to-follow exercises
- provides methods for learning which you can customize according to your needs
- offers ways of integrating accent with acting in various working scenarios

This book does not:

- teach specific accents, rather it offers multiple learning approaches which can be applied to any accent
- replace a one-to-one dialect coach. A coach offers bespoke teaching tailored to individual needs as well as an expert ear. This book offers ways to craft your own process and get closer to your goals

Accent work shouldn't simply be a technical exercise. It's a vital and exciting part of the acting process. This book is designed to help you integrate your work on accents with your work as an actor.

How to use this book

This book is full of practical exercises. A combination of technical information and imaginative descriptions is used to help you connect with speech and accent features.

Pick and choose or do it all!

The book is made up of four parts: Speech, Accent, Acting and Troubleshooting. You can dip in and out, or you could go through from cover to cover, depending on what your aims are, what you're learning or how much time you have. The index and 'Troubleshooting' section can help you decide where to begin.

In Part B, exercises are divided into 'Discovering' and 'Doing' sections so you can prioritize exploration or practice.

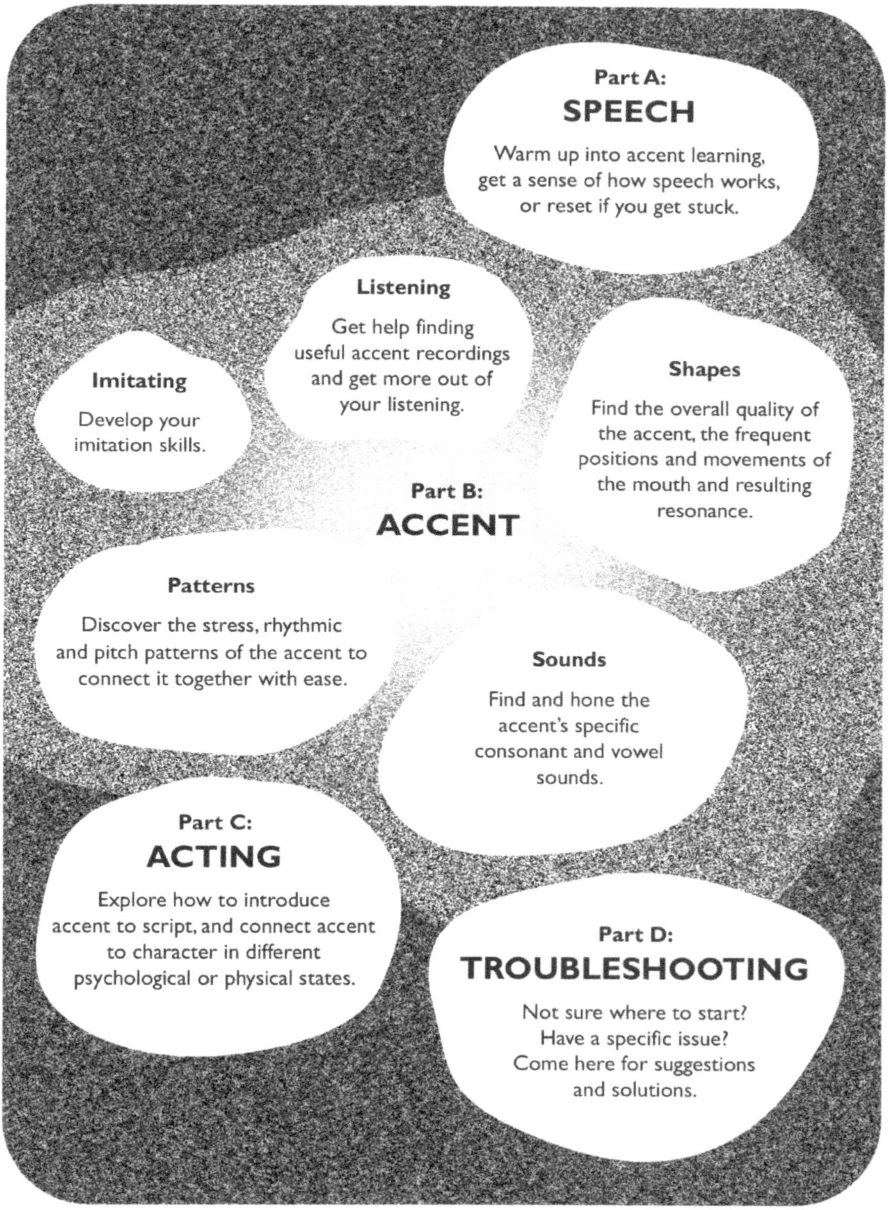

Part A:
SPEECH
Warm up into accent learning, get a sense of how speech works, or reset if you get stuck.

Listening
Get help finding useful accent recordings and get more out of your listening.

Imitating
Develop your imitation skills.

Shapes
Find the overall quality of the accent, the frequent positions and movements of the mouth and resulting resonance.

Part B:
ACCENT

Patterns
Discover the stress, rhythmic and pitch patterns of the accent to connect it together with ease.

Sounds
Find and hone the accent's specific consonant and vowel sounds.

Part C:
ACTING
Explore how to introduce accent to script, and connect accent to character in different psychological or physical states.

Part D:
TROUBLESHOOTING
Not sure where to start? Have a specific issue? Come here for suggestions and solutions.

It can be helpful to explore the same thing from different angles. You may find that you gain more confidence with something once you've explored it using a variety of exercises.

Make notes

It's a good idea to make notes when you're learning an accent so you can remember it. This is especially helpful when working on a script.

These notes could be based on how you discovered an accent feature, what it makes you think of, how it feels to make it or how it changes the word or phrase. Make it memorable. You could:

- write reminders
- record voice notes
- rewrite words so they look more like how they sound, for example, 'lot' becomes 'laht'
- colour-code
- underline
- draw arrows, shapes, symbols and so on

Whenever you discover an accent feature, ask yourself: If you had to mark it down on a page to remind yourself of it without a recording, what would you do?

Test out how well a note works by using it to recreate the accent feature. Can you produce the feature without listening to a recording? If so, that's a helpful note!

Play is the highest form of research.

– Albert Einstein

So, let's play!

Springboard

These exercises can help prepare you for accent learning. They can build positive associations with the work, ease unnecessary tensions and focus the mind.

Exercise: **Shape Your Space**

To create helpful working conditions
You need: something to write with and on (optional)
Make yourself comfortable. When faced with a task, you may feel under pressure and this can stop you from taking things in. Build positive associations with your accent work.

Experiment with what works best for you. Do you prefer a quiet space or one with some background noise? Perhaps light some candles, diffuse some essential oils or grab a blanket if that will put you at ease. Get rid of distractions. Is your phone on silent? Is the door closed? Are you hungry? Are you too cold or too hot?

Sit, stand, lie down, walk around. Anything that allows the body to release and the breath to flow is going to help your focus and comprehension. If you get distracted by internal thoughts, keep something to write with nearby and jot down the thought for later.

Exercise: **Have a Bash!**

To start playing with an accent
You need: a recording device. A dramatic scene or speech you can read easily from the page. A recording of someone speaking in the accent you want to try (optional)
This exercise can be helpful if you don't know where to start, or you feel daunted by accent learning.

First, you're going to split yourself into two people: the actor and the coach. To help, you could give yourself two different walks, divide your room into 'actor's territory' and 'coach's territory', or even give yourself a prop or costume change to make the distinction between your two selves.

Choose an accent to 'have a bash' with. Pick up your scene or speech. It helps to use something with high stakes, like an argument, a declaration of love or a dramatic moment of realization. This can allow you to focus more on acting than on how you sound.

Take a moment to imagine yourself as the actor who is really confident about doing this accent. Now, simply start speaking in the accent as best you can, or at least what you 'imagine' the accent to be. Don't stop! Keep the flow going, even if you feel yourself stumbling or the accent going awry. If you absolutely can't start, have a quick listen to an accent recording, but don't spend too long on it. This isn't about being 'good' at it, it's about 'having a bash'.

Turn on the recording device. Go back and read the scene or speech again, this time committing to the accent and performance with as much enthusiasm as possible.

Remember that this actor playing this part is amazing and has the confidence of Tom Cruise performing all his stunts! Go for it!

Stop the recording. You're now no longer the actor but the coach, so switch hats (literally if this helps). Remember that the coach is there to support the actor and listen objectively to what they're doing. Listen to the recording. Encourage the actor side of yourself – what do you think you did well? What could you work on?

You're going to be asked to 'have a bash' throughout this book, whether it's listening to things in a new way, moving your mouth differently or trying unfamiliar sounds. This exercise encourages you to get 'doing', behave playfully and treat yourself with kindness as you learn.

Exercise: **Zen Master**

To help prepare for listening
Being present when listening reduces the desire to predict what we're going to hear and allows us to focus on how things really are being pronounced.

Find a quiet space. Sit comfortably and either close your eyes or soften their focus. Notice your breathing. Sense the air entering and leaving your body. Is it entering through the nose or the mouth? Are you holding any excessive tension anywhere? Perhaps in the jaw, or the eyes? If so, try to let it go.

Open your awareness to the outside of your body. Listen to the sounds in your space. What do you hear? Which sounds are closest to you, and which are further away? Bring your attention back to your breath. Stay focused on your in-breath and out-breath until you feel calm and ready to begin the work.

Exercise: **Free the Fear**

To practise making mistakes
You need: a recording device. A piece of text (optional)
The actor Willem Dafoe, in a 2020 interview said: 'I always like this idea of trying to fail. . . . Try to make a bad painting. Try to act badly. Try to be lousy in that scene . . . you've got to find ways to let you not worry and be free.'[2]

Although making mistakes is a part of learning, we often feel as though we should be perfect from the start. This exercise takes its cue from Dafoe, making 'failure' a game so we can accept making mistakes.

Start by deciding what 'failing' at learning an accent would be. What would failure look and sound like? You can think about it, make notes, draw pictures, anything that helps.

Just as in **Have a Bash!**, you're now going to split yourself into two people: actor and coach. Choose an accent to try. It could be the one you need to learn, or another. Your task is now to do the absolute worst version of that accent, one that matches your idea of 'wrong'. You can read a scene or speech, or you could improvise by describing something or someone you love.

Turn on the video or voice recorder. Give your performance, committing to the worst version of the accent at a level 10.

Stop the recording. You're now no longer the actor but the coach, so switch hats (literally if this helps!). Listen to the recording as the coach. How well did the actor fail? Did they get everything wrong as they set out to? Did it sound like the accent at all? If so, they might have failed at failure!

This exercise is here to help make mistakes feel more familiar, less important and to lower the stakes of learning.

Part A Speech

The tongue can paint what the eyes can't see.

– Chinese proverb

Part A is all about you. It's an opportunity to explore how you produce speech in your own accent. It's also a place to explore different ways of producing speech and to get yourself ready for working on a new accent.

Part A is a great place to:

- start if you've never learnt an accent before
- go to if you're having trouble with an aspect of the accent in Part B

Why?

- Understanding how *you* speak can be key to understanding how someone *else* does
- Expanding on what you currently do can free you up to imitate someone else

Think of it this way: when training for a marathon, people often do exercise other than running – they swim, they walk and so on. These aren't entirely the same activities, but they all help to achieve the final goal. The same goes for accent learning.

Remember: You can pick and choose which exercises to do. They don't have to be completed in any particular order.

Go to **Part B** if:

- you want to dive straight into listening and discovering an accent's features
- you have a good understanding of your own speech anatomy

Go to **Part C** if:

- you already have a grasp on the accent and want to apply it to text and character work

Your own speech anatomy

We're all different. No two bodies are entirely the same and what a wonderful thing that is! Still, we can tend to compare ourselves unfavourably with others.

So, be kind to yourself. Perhaps your body doesn't look like the bodies in the images in this book. No problem. These are simply representations of how something can be and not in any way depictions of how it should be. Perhaps your body doesn't allow you to move in the way the exercises are suggesting. That's fine. Feel free to explore a different way to make it work for you, and if you simply can't connect with a particular exercise, try a different one!

The vocal tract

The vocal tract is the area inside the body where sound is produced and made into speech. It starts at the **larynx** and ends at the **lips** and **nose**. Everyone's vocal tract is unique and adds to the individual nature of their voice (Figures 1 and 2). These exercises are to:

- help you explore your own vocal tract
- help you learn the names of each part

Exercise: **Car Wash**

To help explore your vocal tract
You need: recording 1 (https://www.bloomsburyonlineresources.com/the-accent-handbook) to guide you through the exercise (optional)
Imagine your head is a car that's booked in for a full wash, inside and out. Start with the outside. Using your fingertips, 'clean' the entire surface of your face. Clean your eyebrows and forehead and explore their different textures. What do they feel like?

Clean your nose, your cheeks and your **jaw**. Check you aren't holding your breath. Let it flow. How many different textures have you discovered with your fingertips? Which parts are hard, and which are softer?

Keep your fingertips on either side of the jaw and open your mouth. You can think of this as opening the boot or trunk of the car. Open and close your mouth and experience the movements. Use your fingertips to explore the **lips**. Feel their textures and how they move when being cleaned. Clean your chin. What does it feel like?

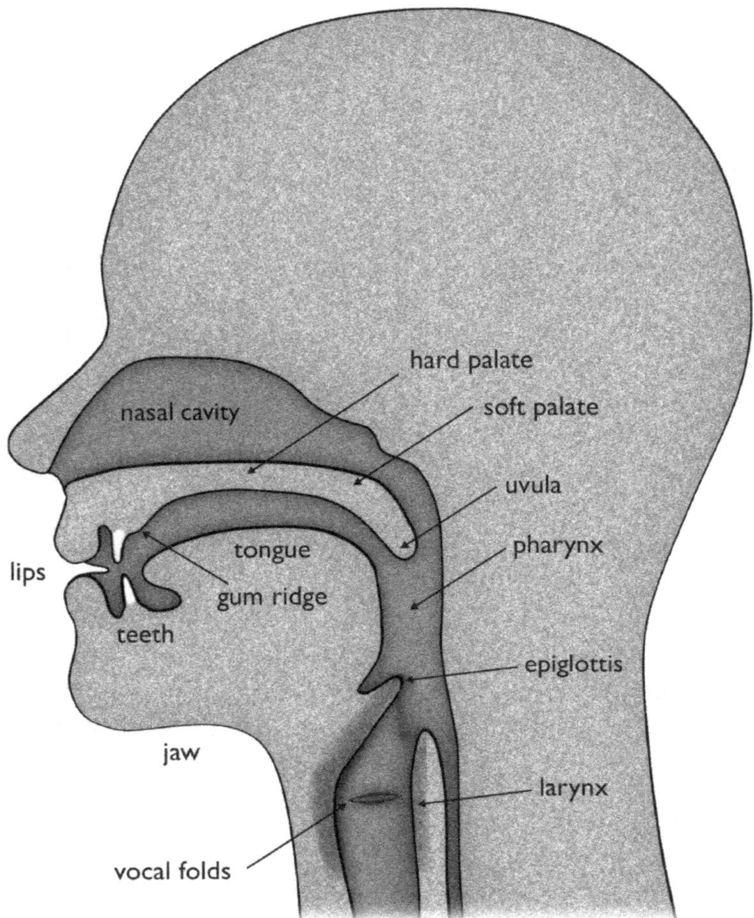

Figure 1 The vocal tract.

Bring your fingers down under your chin to your neck. Very gently, explore and clean the front of your neck. This is where the **larynx** lives, which contains the **vocal folds**. You can't feel your vocal folds, but if you hum, you will feel the result of them vibrating.

Move your attention inside your mouth. Your tongue is the vacuum cleaner. Use the tongue tip to explore and clean every nook and cranny. Clean all your teeth and the spots in between each tooth. Vacuum the roof of the mouth and the floor, underneath your tongue. Keep the breath flowing.

Place the tongue tip behind the top front **teeth** and clean them. Slide the vacuum up to the point where the teeth attach to the gum. This lumpy part above the teeth is called the **gum ridge**. Keep vacuuming back and you will find the **hard palate**. This is hard and slimy; it may feel tickly to vacuum this part. If you can, slide your tongue tip even further back. You may arrive at a point at which the hard palate becomes

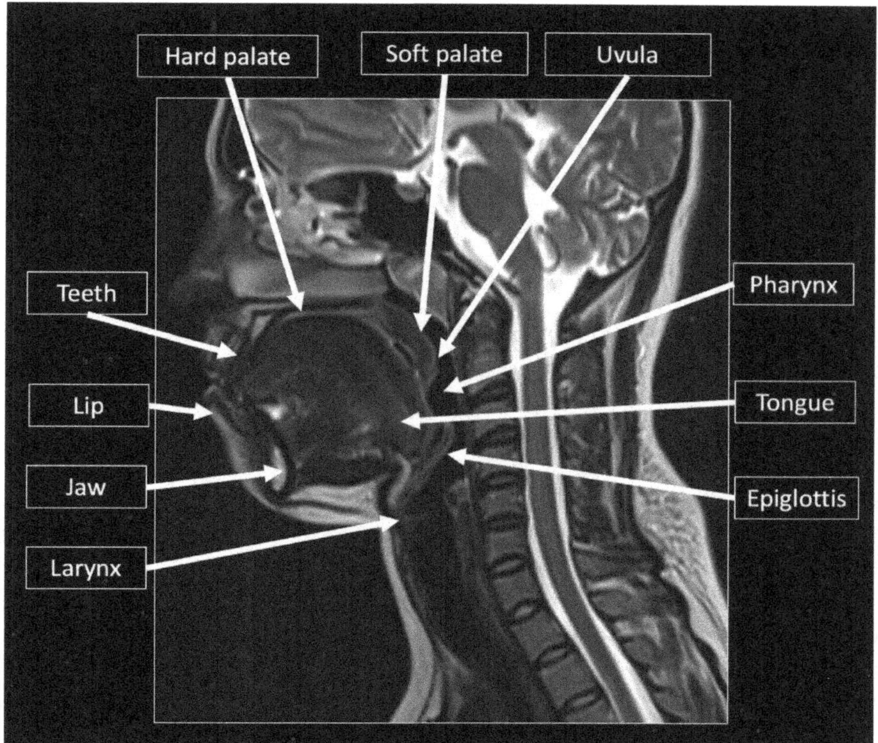

Figure 2 MRI of the vocal tract.

soft and fleshy. This is your **soft palate** (some of us can't slide the tongue tip this far back).

To explore the **uvula** (the dangly bit), release the tongue tip down so it rests behind the bottom front teeth and imagine the air from the vacuum coming from the back of the mouth. Breathe out through your mouth and bring the uvula to the back of the tongue to create a trill-like sound. You can explore this on an in-breath as well as an out-breath (as if you've vacuumed up a sock!).

Different parts of the vocal tract are written in **bold** and are referenced throughout this book. You can see them in Figures 1 and 2. If any parts or terms are unfamiliar to you, spend some time re-exploring them. The better you know your vocal tract, the easier accent work can be.

Exercise: **The Michelangelo**

To help learn the parts of the vocal tract
You need: diagram of the vocal tract with labels, MRI or photograph
Something to draw with and on, or modelling clay, plasticine or dough
Sometimes the simple act of drawing something can help to remember it better, so why not try copying or tracing one of the diagrams of the vocal tract on pp. 14 and 15

and labelling it? If colour appeals to you, use different shades for the various parts to help make them stand out.

Alternatively, take something you can mould like modelling clay, plasticine or dough, and create your own 3D model of the vocal tract. Why not put your masterpiece near where you work so you can refer to it?

Exercise: **Mirror, Mirror on the Wall**

To help explore your vocal tract
You need: a mirror
Look in the mirror and bring your focus to your mouth. Look at its shape and colours. Look at your **lips** and watch as you move them around. What kind of shapes can you make with them? Gently bite down on your bottom lip, if that's an option for you, and notice the textures. Let the breath flow.

Open your mouth and look at your **teeth**. Run the tip of your tongue over your top and bottom teeth to notice how they feel. Bring your top and bottom teeth together. What sound do they make when they touch? Compare the textures of your lips and teeth.

Look at your **tongue**. Move it and watch it morph into different shapes. Are there different parts to your tongue, different colours and textures? How many shapes can you create with it? Can you move the back of your tongue independently from the tip? Check you aren't holding your breath.

Try looking at the roof of your mouth, your **hard palate**, by tilting your head back slightly. What does it look like? Bring the tip of your tongue up to touch it and notice how it feels.

If you can, bring the tongue tip back even further to the **soft palate**. What does it feel like? Can you see the soft palate? Is it possible to move it? Try yawning. Can you see the soft palate raise?

Look at the **uvula**, the dangling 'little grape' at the end of your soft palate. Can you touch it with the back of your tongue?

There are a few parts of the vocal tract that can't be seen in the mirror. First, the **nasal passage**. If you had a tiny camera that you put up one of your nostrils, you would be in the nasal passage. If you then continued to move your camera through the nasal passage and down into your throat (a horrible thought for some!), you would see the **pharynx**, the back wall of the throat. If you went down even further, you would be able to glimpse the **larynx** and the **vocal folds.**

Look in the mirror and swallow. If you notice any movement in the front of your neck, you're seeing your larynx moving up and down inside your body.

Exercise: **Name Game**

To help learn the parts of the vocal tract
Learning the names of objects can be helpful in gaining a greater familiarity with them and their use. If you like singing, channel your inner child at a party and hum the

tune of 'Heads, Shoulders, Knees and Toes'. Using the same tune, sing these lyrics instead:

> Vocal folds, tongue, lips and teeth, lips and teeth,
> Vocal folds, tongue, lips and teeth, lips and teeth,
> Uvula, soft palate, hard palate, gum ridge,
> Vocal folds, tongue, lips and teeth, lips and teeth!

As you sing, point to the parts of your own vocal tract! Could it catch on?

The articulators

The articulators are the parts of the vocal tract responsible for shaping sound into speech. Some articulators are immovable: **teeth** (hopefully), **gum ridge** and **hard palate.** Other articulators are moveable:

- **jaw**
- **lips**
- **tongue**
- **soft palate**
- **uvula**
- **vocal folds**

(For the purposes of this work we will consider the **pharynx** to be immovable; however, in reality it is able to move a little). The following exercises are to help you:

- become better acquainted with your articulators
- explore the possible positions and movements of each articulator
- discover your own habitual positions and movements for each articulator, which contribute to your own accent

Jaw

The jaw is the only moveable bone in the skull. Its primary function is to bite, chew and grind down food but it's also involved in shaping speech. Why consider the jaw for accent work? The positions and movements of a speaker's jaw can add to the overall **quality** or **'character'** of their sound. People use their jaws in different ways when speaking. Some lower it slightly, while others drop it further. Some hardly move it at all, while others move it often. Noticing and adopting the movements and positions of the jaw for the accent you're learning can help you get closer to the new sound (Figure 3).

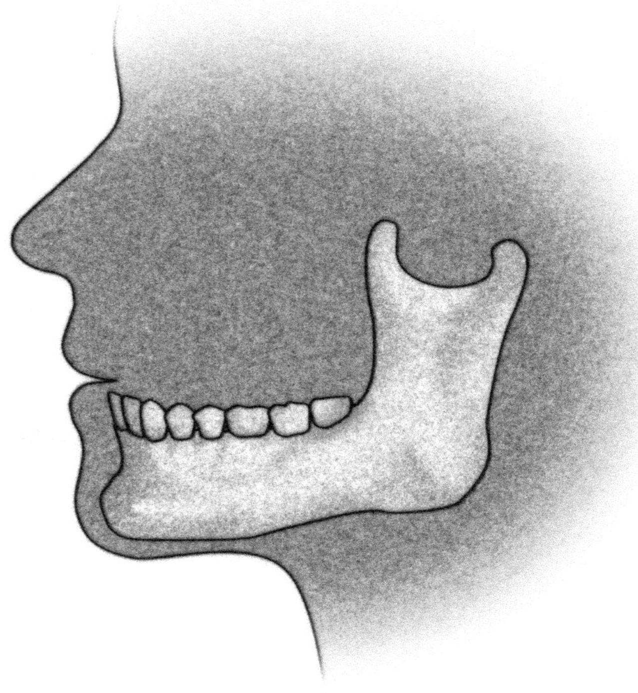

Figure 3 Jawbone.

Exercise: **Jaw Explore**

To help explore possible jaw positions and movements
Find your cheekbones using your fingertips. Bring your fingertips just under your cheekbones, then slide them back towards your ears and you'll find the top of the jawbone, or jaw hinge. With your fingertips resting on the hinge, gently lower your jaw. Breathe. Raise your jaw. Breathe. Move slowly between lowering and raising your jaw so that your mouth opens and closes and track the movement with your fingertips. Check you aren't holding your breath and stop at the first sign of discomfort. Perhaps your jaw has a smooth ride up and down, or perhaps you feel some clicking. Everyone's jaw hinge is different – no jaw journey is the same!

Once you've explored up and down, explore some sideways movement. Slowly move your jaw from right to left, letting your breath flow.

Explore bringing your jaw forward and back (if this is a possibility for you). Try any other positions or movements that feel interesting to you. Different accents have different positions and movements, so exploring all possibilities can be useful.

Exercise: **Your Jaw**

To help notice your own jaw positions and movements
You need: a way of videoing yourself

Film yourself talking for a minute or two. You could talk about where you grew up, your favourite food or what you're doing at the weekend. Aim to speak as you usually would and try to forget the camera is there. Watch the video back and look at your jaw. Focus on two things: the **positions** it finds and the **movements** it makes.

Positions

Overall, how much does it open? Do you see a lot of space in your mouth as you speak, or are the top and bottom teeth mostly close together?

Movements

Overall, how often does it move? Is it **moving** a lot, or is it mostly **still**? If it's difficult to tell try speaking again, placing a finger lightly on your chin to monitor the movement.

Make a note of your findings. These observations may help you understand the difference between your jaw shapes and a new accent's.

Exercise: **Jaw Jive**

To help explore how varying jaw movement can affect your sound
You need: some text, some music options

Imagine your jaw is going to a school dance. Different songs will affect how much the jaw moves when it dances along. Start off with a slow dance that needs very little movement (you can even play some slow music to set the mood). Start to move the jaw in sync with the music, letting the movements be small and smooth. Keep breathing.

Switch to an upbeat song which would get those on the dance floor bouncing around and which calls for more jaw movement (you can also make this change with your music). Explore some more energetic movement with your jaw. Raise and lower it; move it side to side (carefully). Keep breathing.

Now bring this into your reading of the text. First, use very little jaw movement as you speak. Does it affect your sound? Does the sound quality change in any way?

Use much more movement and notice how you sound. Play with opening and closing. Does it affect your sound? Shift between a little and a lot of movement and monitor any differences in your sound. Which feels most comfortable and familiar to you? Note down any observations.

Lips

The lips are one of the gateways to the vocal tract (the nose is the other). They're made up of two rings of muscles: the inner ring and the outer ring. These rings are responsible for creating different shapes and movements which we use for speech. Why consider the lips for accent work? The shapes a speaker makes with their lips can add to the overall **quality of their sound**. People use their lips in different ways. Some speakers move their lips a lot, while others hardly do at all. Some create lots of round shapes with their lips, while others tend to spread them wide to create a flat line. Noticing and adopting the movements and shapes of the lips for the accent you're learning can help you get closer to the new sound.

Exercise: **The Jim Carrey**

To help explore possible lip shapes and movements
You need: a mirror
Think of your face as being made of super flexible rubber, like the actor and comedian Jim Carrey's.

In front of a mirror, start to move your lips in different ways, noticing all the different positions you can move them into. Check you aren't holding your breath. Try to move your lips in a way you've never done before. Can you move your top lip only? Bottom lip only? What is the most ridiculous shape you can make?

Exercise: **Your Lips**

To explore your habitual lip shapes and movements
You need: a way of filming yourself
Film yourself on your device talking for a minute or two. Speak about a place you'd really like to travel to, or your favourite childhood memory. Try to forget you're recording. Watch the video back and observe your lips. Focus on two things, their overall shapes and their movements.

Shapes

What shapes do they make? Are they creating lots of round shapes? Or are they mainly flat and straight? Are they doing both, or neither? The chances are you will notice a few different shapes being made, but what do you see most frequently?

Movements

Do they move a lot when you talk or are they relatively still? Could you understand what you're saying without the sound, or are you more like a ventriloquist? Make a note of your findings with a doodle or writing. These observations may help you understand the difference between your lip shapes and those of the new accent.

Exercise: **Lip Gymnastics**

To help explore how different lip shapes can affect your sound
You need: a mirror and some text

In front of a mirror, perform your best pout. This is achieved by bringing the lip corners away from the teeth. Try to avoid creating lots of tension in the lips as you do this, think of a 'loose pout' (Figure 4).

With the lips like this, speak some text. Try to keep your lip corners in this shape. Does this affect your sound? How? Are some sounds easier to make than others? Does this feel comfortable, or do you feel like you're speaking through someone else's mouth?

Now, as well as bringing the lip corners out, away from your teeth, bring the top and bottom lips together to create a tiny circle. You can think of the action of blowing a kiss, but don't let the lips quite touch (Figure 5).

With the lips in this shape, speak your text out loud. Does this affect your sound? How? Are some sounds easier to make than others? Does this feel comfortable for you, or is this shape one you don't usually make?

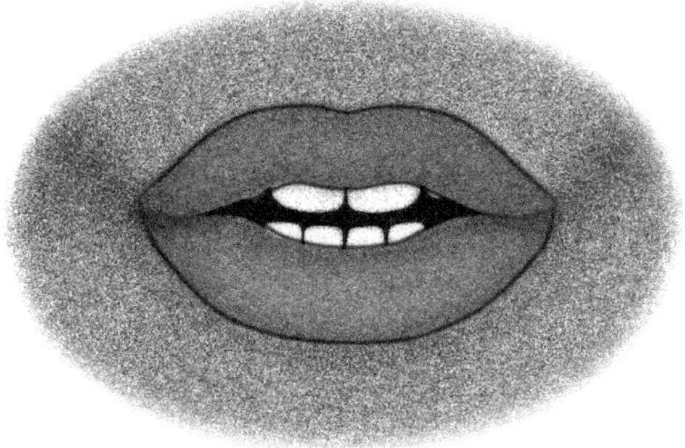

Figure 4 Pouty lips.

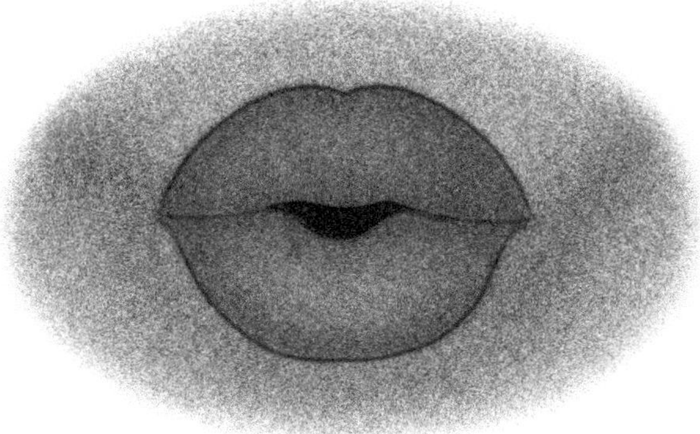

Figure 5 Rounded lips.

Move between the two shapes and notice if and how your sound changes.

Release the lips and bring the lip corners away from each other, towards the ears. Try to create a straight line with them, rather than bringing them up into a smile (Figure 6).

With your lips in this shape, speak your text. Does this affect your sound? How? Does this feel comfortable or are you longing to return to more rounded shapes? Move between these three shapes and notice how your sound changes. Blow raspberries to release any tension you may be holding in your lips and allow them to remain released (Figure 7).

Speak your text without creating any particular shapes at all. The lips may close for some sounds but try to keep your lip corners released throughout. Does this affect your sound? How? Explore all these different shapes again as you speak your text. Can you find varying degrees of each shape? Which shapes feel most familiar to you?

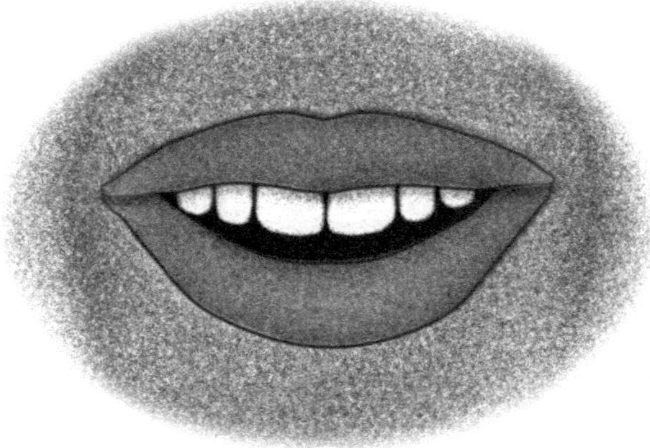

Figure 6 Spread lips.

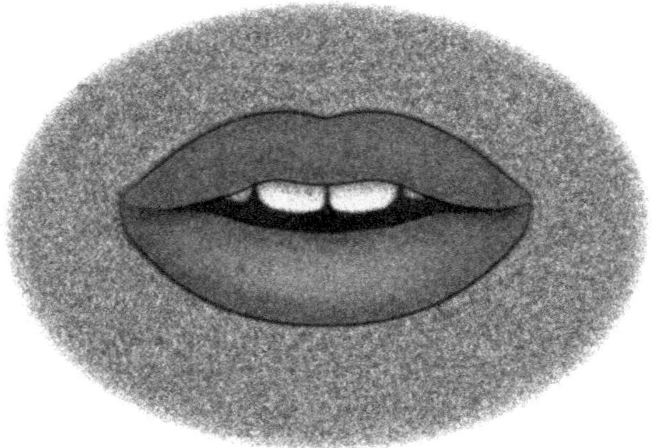

Figure 7 Unrounded lips.

Exercise: **Getting Lippy with It**

To help explore how varying lip movement can affect your sound
You need: some text

Speak your text. What is the minimum lip movement you can make while still being understood? Does this affect your sound? How?

Speak your text as if you're trying to get someone on the other side of a soundproof window to understand it. This will require maximum lip movement. Does this affect your sound? How? Move between minimum and maximum lip movement and notice any changes to your sound.

Tongue

The tongue is made up of different muscles that allow it to move in various ways to make speech sounds. How a speaker moves their tongue determines a lot about their accent. This is focused on more in **Part B**. Gaining more awareness of your tongue and how it moves is a useful step to taking on another accent (Figure 8).

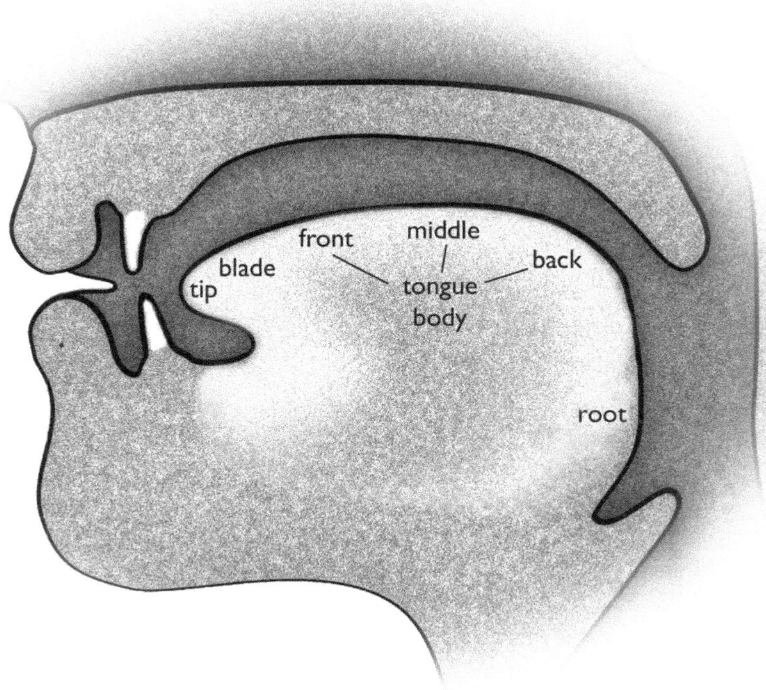

Figure 8 Tongue – side view.

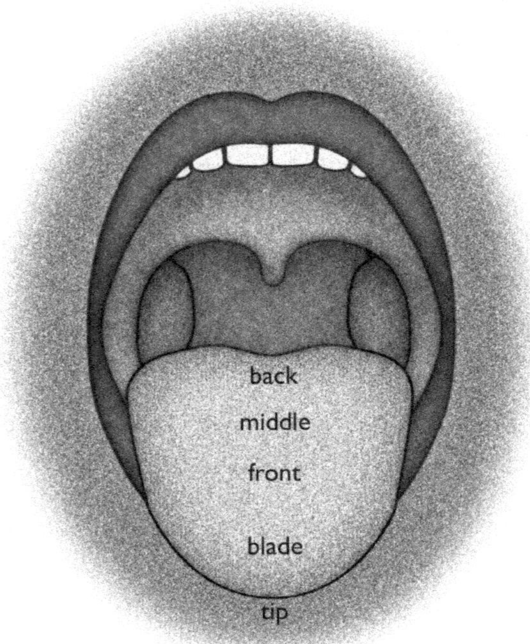

Figure 9 Tongue – front view.

Different parts of the tongue help to create different sounds. Rather than thinking of the tongue as a whole, it can be useful to think of it as made up of different parts (Figure 9).

To remember the parts of the tongue, why not try **The Michelangelo** exercise (p. 15) and either draw or sculpt it?

Exercise: **Tongue Tour**

To help explore the parts of the tongue
You need: a mirror

In front of a mirror, slide your tongue out of your mouth to see as much of it as feels comfortable. Focus on the tongue **tip**, the very front edge of your tongue. Gently bite down on the tip to help focus your attention there.

Now move back a little to the **blade** of your tongue. When does the tip become the blade? There is no official dotted line that runs between the two but, generally speaking, the blade is 'the bit behind the tip'! Bite on the tip and then slowly slide the tongue forward. As soon as the tongue gets a little thicker, you're biting on the blade.

Behind the blade is the tongue body, composed of three parts: the front, middle and back. The **front** is directly behind the blade. Gently bite the tip, the blade, then the front of the tongue body. Which part is most sensitive?

It becomes increasingly difficult (and then impossible) to explore much further back by biting, so look in the mirror. The **middle of the tongue body** is behind the front, and the **back of the tongue body** is behind the middle. This is the furthest back you can see in the mirror. Does the tongue look the same all the way back or does the colour and/or texture change?

You can't see the **tongue root** using a mirror, as it goes down your throat. Place a finger under your chin and poke the fleshy part. Keep your finger there and swallow. Do you feel something tense? This is the tongue root moving.

Exercise: **Track the Tongue**

To help build awareness and sensation of the tongue and its movements
You need: a clean finger, something to write with and on
Touch your tongue with your finger. Notice how your tongue reacts to having your finger on it. Move your finger around to feel different parts of the tongue; the sides, underneath, the front edge and so on. Notice whether your tongue starts to move as you do this.

Lay your finger lengthways on your tongue, only placing your fingertip as far back as feels comfortable. Start to move your tongue up and down, then forward and back, sensing the movements with your finger. Make different shapes with your tongue, keeping your finger on it. What different shapes can you make?

Make a continuous vowel sound – OO, or EE, for instance. How has the tongue shaped itself to create this sound? Make another vowel sound and notice how the tongue moves to shape it.

Make different vowel sounds and move from one to another, feeling the movement of the tongue with your finger. Where is the tongue going in the mouth and what shapes is it making to produce these sounds? Note down any observations or discoveries.

Exercise: **Tongue Drums**

To help explore the different parts of the tongue
Place the tip of your tongue behind your top front teeth and make a type of T sound with the tip there. It may help to think of this sound as a little 'explosion'.

Now place the blade of your tongue on the gum ridge and create a type of T sound there. Does it have a slightly different quality to the sound you created with the tip of the tongue behind the top teeth? Move between the two to notice any differences.

Bring the tongue tip down behind your bottom front teeth and bring the front of the tongue body up to the hard palate and make a type of explosion here. It may sound like a type of T sound, or a type of K sound.

Bring the middle of the tongue body to the soft palate and create an explosion there. This may sound like a type of K sound.

Bring the back of the tongue body to the uvula and create an explosion there. This may sound like a type of K sound.

Bring the root of the tongue back until it touches the pharynx (back of the throat) and create an explosion there. This may also sound like a type of K sound.

Explore the different explosions you can make with different parts of the tongue in different places – play your tongue drums!

Exercise: **Tongue Tip Travel**

To help explore different tongue tip positions

Take the phrase: *Tom was talking to twenty-two cacti.* Say this phrase with the tongue tip **behind the top front teeth** for each of the Ts in bold. Notice how it sounds and feels. Say the phrase with the tip of the tongue on the **gum ridge** for each of the Ts. Notice how it sounds and feels. Say the phrase with the tip of the tongue on the **hard palate**. Notice how it sounds and feels. Which position feels and sounds most familiar to you?

Exercise: **Weightlifting**

To help explore different tongue body positions
You need: some text

Imagine you have a (clean) pound coin balanced on the back of your tongue body. Allow the idea of weight to bring the back of the tongue body down as far as it can go.

Speak your text. Can you keep the back of the tongue body in this low position throughout? How does this affect your sound?

Place the imaginary coin on the middle of the tongue body and raise it up to the soft palate. Can you keep the middle of the tongue body high as you speak your text? How does this affect your sound?

Can you place the coin on the front of the tongue body and raise it towards the top front teeth? Speak your text in this position. How does this affect your sound?

Speak your text, starting with the back of the tongue body down, as far as it can go. Slowly raise the middle up towards the uvula and then bring the front of the tongue body up to the top front teeth. Note any changes to your sound.

Exercise: **Heavy Tongue, Light Tongue**

To help explore different movement qualities of the tongue
You need: some text

Think of your tongue being so heavy that it's practically unable to move from the floor of your mouth. Really feel its weight in your mouth. Speak your text with your tongue in this heavy position. Notice how it sounds and feels.

Think of your tongue being as light as a helium balloon, floating around near the roof of your mouth. Speak your text. Notice how it sounds and feels.

Move between a heavy tongue and a light tongue. Which movement quality feels most familiar to you? Note down any discoveries.

Exercise: **Animal Tongue**

To help explore different movement qualities of the tongue
You need: some text

Pick an animal. Think about the movement qualities of that animal. Is it fast or slow? Light or heavy? Does it take up space or make itself small?

Imagine your tongue is that animal. Move it around your mouth with these movement qualities. Speak some text, letting these qualities affect the speed, weight, and size of your tongue as you form the words. Notice how it sounds and feels.

Pick a different animal and repeat the exercise. Notice whether different movement qualities change the sound in any way. Note down any discoveries.

Soft palate

The soft palate can raise and lower to open and close the passage to the nose, which is essential for breathing and swallowing. It's also responsible for the creation of speech sounds. For some sounds, the soft palate lowers to send air through the nose. For others it raises, directing air through the mouth (Figure 10).

In addition, the overall position of the soft palate can influence the resonant quality of your voice. Certain accents have a lower soft palate resting position, while others have a higher resting position, so being able to manipulate it is extremely useful for taking on someone else's sound quality.

Exercise: **Gasp!**

To help feel your soft palate

Find a comfortable position, either sitting or standing and focus on your breath.

Imagine you've been told some really exciting news that makes you gasp with glee. Try gasping a few times and notice the sensation. Do you feel cold air hitting the back of your throat as you gasp? The cold air is hitting your soft palate, and as you gasp it lifts up.

Move between resting and gasping with glee to feel the soft palate rise. Doing this too much may make you feel light-headed, so take breaks.

Exercise: **Hoist the Sail**

To help explore different soft palate positions
You need: a mirror

Say the word 'sing' and hold onto the end of it: sinnnnngggggg. Open your mouth and look in the mirror as you make this sound. It's likely that you will see the middle of the tongue body raised. It's touching the soft palate, which sends air through your nose. To test this, give your nose a pinch as you make the NG and notice how the sound stops.

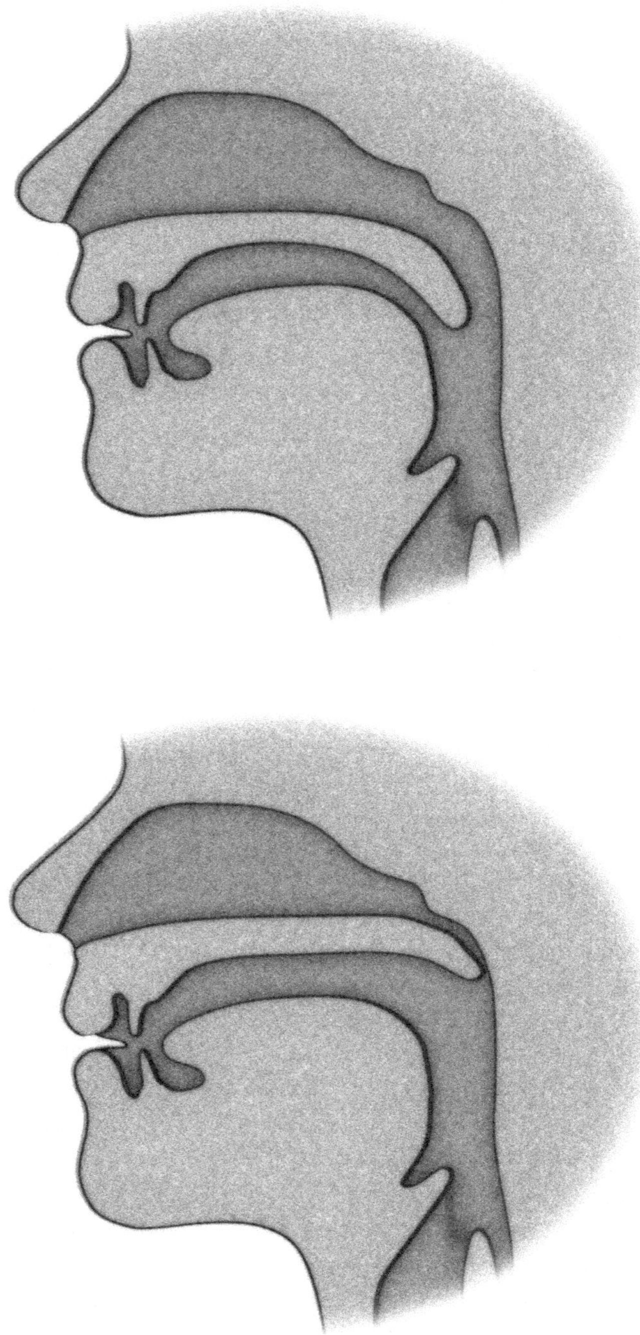

Figure 10 Soft palate lowered and raised.

Say the word 'sing' again, and end it with a 'GUH' sound, lengthening the UH element: singuuuuuuuuuh.

Look in the mirror. You might see the tongue move down and the soft palate raise as you release the 'G'. The chances are, you've now redirected the air through the mouth. Think of a yawn and you might feel it raise even more. Try pinching your nose as you make the UH. If your soft palate is completely raised, pinching your nose should not affect the sound in any way. If it does, make an even stronger 'GUH' sound to lift the soft palate further. Move between an 'NG' and a 'GUH' and trace the movement of the soft palate in the mirror. You've lowered and raised it.

To find a mid-position (between completely lowered and raised), start with an NG and move to a GUH slowly. As you do, keep the soft palate low, as close to the middle of the tongue body as possible. Use the mirror to help you. The resulting sound can be described as **nasalized**. Pinch your nose as you make the UH. Do you notice that the sound doesn't stop completely but the quality changes slightly? If so, you've identified a mid-position. If it doesn't, work to lower the soft palate towards the tongue but don't quite let it touch and pinch your nose again to check whether there is a change in sound quality.

Part B Accent

Part B is all about the **accent** you're wanting to learn. It's the place for **discovering** the accent's features and **doing** them. It's a great place to:

- learn how to find useful accent recordings and get more out of them
- gain experience of imitating
- discover the features of the new accent
- explore ways of taking on the accent features
- start putting the features of the accent together

Remember: You can pick and choose which exercises to do. They don't have to be completed in any particular order.

Go to **Part A** if:

- you've never learnt an accent before
- you're having trouble with an aspect of the accent in Part B

Go to **Part C** if:

- you've discovered and explored the accent's features
- you are ready to apply accent to text and act in the accent

Listening

Listening is a positive act. You have to put yourself out to listen.

– David Hockney

Listening is crucial to accent learning. Trying to perform an accent without listening to it leaves you guessing at, rather than really knowing the accent, playing the idea rather than the reality. You wouldn't set off for an appointment without the address!

Having a great recording of the accent with a clear idea of what to listen out for is the first step to finding confidence, consistency and accuracy. The more you listen, the more familiar the sounds will become. Still, when you're under pressure for an audition or you're nervous about the accent in question, it can be surprisingly tempting to skip or subconsciously avoid listening.

This guide will help you find useful recordings and get the most out of them. The section includes:

- what to look for
- where to find recordings
- less helpful recordings
- how to generate your own recording
- how to listen
- how to imitate

What to search for

Figuring out what you want can be a key step towards building your character. You might feel it helpful to do some character and text work before you look for a recording. If so, the **'Accent and character'** section of **Part C** (p. 160) has exercises to help.

The most reliable, useful recording of an accent you will ever find is a recording (audio or video) of someone talking, unselfconsciously, for a good length of time without too much interruption. Search for:

- speakers born in the area you're looking at or who have had the accent from a young age and spent a lot of time in the area

- speakers talking conversationally, without excess interruption
- a good quality recording without distracting background sounds or music

Clarify your aims and needs. You could be wanting to:

- audition for a role
- play a role
- improve your accent work generally

If you're about to **audition for or play a role**, try to find a speaker as much like the character as possible. You may not have much information from the casting breakdown, production or script, but it's worth narrowing the search for yourself to find detail. Consider:

- location (country, region, town, borough)
- age
- gender
- ethnicity
- social or economic background
- age of the recording (if the character is from another era)

If you want to **improve your accent work generally**, consider searching for speakers who reflect roles you'd like to play.

Where to search

The internet has gifted us access to millions of accent recordings from all over the world, past and present. With such a huge search field it's helpful to find specific ways of uncovering those golden recordings just when you need them. The most helpful recordings tend to be found in the following:

- accent and dialect databases (a list follows on p. 35)
- oral histories
- interviews
- documentaries
- lectures/talks
- podcasts
- talk radio

Putting these terms into your internet search engine can help narrow your search quickly and helpfully.

Looking up interviews of notable people from the area can be a shortcut to a good recording, especially from:

- politicians
- athletes
- artists
- writers
- entertainers

YouTube, Vimeo and other video sites

Video sites are vast repositories of accents, but make sure your search terms work for you. Consult the 'What to look for' section and **Search Party** exercise for guidance.

International Dialects of English Archive

Created by Paul Meier, this website contains recordings of accents of English from all over the world.

British Library

Many different recordings of UK accents are stored on this website, both contemporary and historic.

American Library of Congress

An extensive archive of recordings from the United States, both contemporary and historic.

WAAPA Accent and Dialect Collection

A website containing over 380 accent recordings from 68 countries of origin.

The Accent Handbook Recordings

Audio of speakers with various accents accompanies this book (https://www.blo omsburyonlineresources.com/the-accent-handbook).

Exercise: **Search Party**

To help find useful examples
You need: something to write with and on, access to the internet
Everyone has their own way of researching. However, if you find yourself getting lost, this exercise suggests ways of parsing out the task and increasing the chances of finding useful recordings.

Write down any information you have about the accent you're wanting to learn. This could include information on the era, the relationships and the action. List facts about the setting of the piece such as geographical location and immediate settings such as interiors and exteriors. List any unfamiliar words, grammar or vocabulary that seems to be written in dialect; for example, 'I'm finna' or 'y'alright hen?' List all the facts about the character you're playing, such as age, gender, ethnicity, family, friends, education, career, amount of travelling done and places lived. Use the casting breakdown, the script or audition sides and any information you've been given by production.

Let's say you've landed the role of Eddie Carbone in *A View from the Bridge* by Arthur Miller. You know from the script and the casting breakdown:

- New York, Brooklyn, Italian-American neighbourhood, 1950s
- male, roughly middle-aged, longshoreman so working class, second-generation Sicilian so born in America, but parents were Sicilian

Using this information, create a recording wish list:

- Brooklyn
- male
- roughly middle-aged (not too young or elderly)
- Italian-American or specifically Sicilian
- working class
- from the 1950s

Don't worry about finding the perfect recording containing everything on your wish list. The list is there to put detail into your search. Enter the terms on your wish list into an internet search engine in different combinations. If you know little about the area and its people, start more generally:

- Brooklyn documentary
- New York 1950s documentary
- Brooklyn oral history project
- list of Italian-Americans (then search for interviews with the New Yorkers)

If you want to dive straight into the accent, you could be more specific:

- Brooklyn local man interview
- Italian New Yorker interview/documentary
- Sicilian-American interview
- New York longshoreman interview/documentary
- Italian-American podcast

You could also go to one of the websites which hold databases of voice, accent and dialect recordings from different parts of the world, as listed in the 'Where to search' section. When searching and listening, ask yourself:

- Is the speaker roughly the right age bracket?
- Does their background roughly fit?
- Is the recording quality good enough?

You don't have to say yes to all these questions, but they will keep your search focused.

Less helpful recordings

If the following types of recordings are the only ones available, use them. However, it's worth listening to these with a critical ear as they could be misleading:

'How to do X accent' tutorials from the internet

There may be generalizations, inaccuracies or out-of-date information in these tutorials depending on when they were made and by whom.

People 'teaching' their own accent

Speakers of an accent are not necessarily experts when it comes to teaching its features. They can exaggerate when demonstrating and use generalizations. It's more helpful to listen to a recording of them speaking about something else.

Actors performing an accent

Even if they seem convincing, they're doing a 'translation' of the accent and things may get lost. It's more helpful to go right to the source by listening to someone who speaks with the accent every day.

How to generate your own accent recording

A great option is to record someone yourself. The following recording material is available in full in Appendix B on p. 183.

Vowel sentences

By recording these sentences, you will have a sense of how the speaker pronounces their vowel sounds.

Consonant sentences

These sentences contain certain consonant sounds that are useful to focus on as they vary considerably in pronunciation between accents. They can also be pronounced differently depending on where they are in a word or sentence.

Ghost Ship

This story contains all the vowel and consonant sounds put together in connected speech. It allows you to hear how the speaker pronounces their sounds and words in full flow. It can also help to reveal interesting pronunciations which weren't covered by the consonant or vowel sentences.

Free speech

Do you have a reading voice? Almost everyone does. The 'Free speech' section gives a sense of the speaker's accent in conversation, without the pressure of reading. Record a conversation with your speaker and ask them open questions to get them talking for longer.

If you're studying an accent with a first language other than English, ask your speaker to answer a question or two in their first language. This can help you notice which pronunciation features they're bringing into English.

FAQs

How do I know if the speaker has a good example of the accent?

Become better acquainted with the accent by researching the area, listening to local radio or finding documentaries which feature speakers of the accent.

Find a few recordings and listen for similarities between speakers. If four out of five speakers do the same specific thing, the chances are it's a feature of the accent.

Should I pick just one recording or a variety of recordings?

Using a variety can help you check that the example is typical of the accent and can increase your understanding of the range of features speakers may have. If you're clear about your aims and needs you might choose to settle on one recording, especially if you've discovered a lot of variation in the accent and need to narrow it down.

I am learning an accent where English is the second language, but the recordings vary so widely. Where do I start?

Speakers of English as a second language can vary in their pronunciation depending on:

- where and how the speaker learnt English
- where their teacher was from
- how familiar they are with the English language
- where they have lived or spent significant time outside of their home country

Find a speaker who has a similar relationship with the English language to that of your character. For example, if your character has only just arrived in England, find a speaker who has lived mostly in their home country. If your character lives in America, try to find someone who learnt English from an American.

Listen to the speaker's first language. You may not understand it but this can work to your advantage as you won't be distracted by what they're saying. Listen to language patterns or for any sounds that jump out at you. Usually, you will hear at least some features from the first language transferred into their pronunciation of English.

Should I pick a 'strong' example or a 'softer' example?

It depends on your needs and what is being asked of you. Listening to a 'strong' example can be a good starting point as it can help highlight differences between your accent and the new accent.

If you've been specifically asked to do a 'light' version of the accent but you're totally unfamiliar with it, it can be helpful to listen to 'strong' speakers first. Use the 'strong' example to help you pick out a lighter speaker. What is a 'strong' accent? Either:

- It contains many of the features we may expect to hear from that accent, either sounds or dialect terms or phrases.
- It contains sounds that differ from a 'standard' accent. For example, due to accent bias, some may describe an accent as 'strong' in the UK if it differs widely from Received Pronunciation, an accent that has been held in high regard over the years. However, if it contains similar features to the standard, some might consider it a 'soft' example.
- A 'strong' second language accent might contain more of the speaker's first language sounds than a 'softer' one.

If you're unsure, it's worth asking someone familiar with the accent whether they think the example is 'strong'.

How to listen

You already know how to listen. Everyone with the ability to hear listens all day long. However, we're often multitasking as we listen, processing what someone's said, anticipating what they're going to say and finding a reply to keep the conversation flowing. While this may serve you very well in everyday life, learning an accent requires a slightly different form of listening.

The following exercises suggest various ways to listen for accent learning and provide tips to help you get the most out of a recording. Try them and see what works for you.

Detach from distractions

Cast your eyes down or close them, use headphones or find a quiet space. This can help you to focus more on what you hear.

Release your jaw and let the breath flow

This helps you access your auditory cortex (the part of your brain which processes sound).

Listen repeatedly

When first exposed to something new, you're often just taking in the experience. You might not take anything specific away from the first listen other than roughly what the speaker has said. Listening again allows you to get past the content of the speech and the overall sound so you can start picking up on specifics.

Listen silently at first

Try listening to your recording at least twice without imitating. If you speak too early, you might reproduce your own habitual sounds, or what you 'think' you heard after a brief listen. Keep a notepad nearby so you can scribble down what you notice before imitating.

Listen or watch

Some get more out of watching a video of an accent speaker rather than just listening to the audio. Others prefer to focus solely on sound. Do whatever you find most helpful and if you're not sure, experiment.

Exercise: **Don't Fight the Fidget!**

To help focus when listening to the accent

For some, listening is easiest when fully focused on the task without any distractions and without doing anything else simultaneously. For others, it can be more useful to add another activity to help relieve excess energy. This can free the mind to take in the sounds.

If you fit into the second category, or if you're unsure and want to discover what works for you, here are some suggestions:

- Move about your space.
- Tap your hand, foot or pencil.
- Cook.
- Fold laundry.
- Knit.
- Play with modelling clay, dough or plasticine.
- Colour something in.
- Knot or braid string.
- Cut shapes out of paper.
- Doodle.
- Make some marks on the page that relate to what you're hearing – dots, dashes, lines, blobs, shapes and so on.

Doing something enjoyable while listening to the accent can build positive associations with the sounds, shapes and patterns you're hearing. Listening 'unconsciously' while doing other things is a great way of becoming more familiar with the accent without getting overwhelmed.

Exercise: **First Impressions**

To start making observations about the accent
You need: an accent recording (audio only), something to write with and on
This exercise offers an initial way of listening to and making observations about the accent. Before you play the recording, you could do the exercises **Zen Master** or **Don't Fight the Fidget!** to help you focus.

Release the jaw and the breath and play the recording once through. Just listen, don't copy. Consider what went through your head as you listened. Was it what they were saying, how they were saying it or a bit of both? Did any other thoughts crop up? If so, acknowledge them, even jot them down if that helps, and put them aside.

Listen again, focusing solely on how they're speaking and jot down anything you notice. Use descriptive words, shapes, pictures or anything else. Look at what you've noted. These are your first impressions of the accent and are a valuable starting point.

You might have noticed something about the rhythm or pitch. If so, you could head to **Patterns** (p. 56). Perhaps you noted down words with interesting sounds in them. If so, go to **Sounds** (p. 74) to focus on vowels and consonants. Maybe you noticed the overall quality of the accent, in which case head to **Shapes** (p. 47).

Perhaps you have opinions or judgements of the accent in your notes. Confront these now. Biases are inevitable but remember the job: to embody another's experience. Holding on to bias can be a barrier to achieving this.

Imitating

Those who do not want to imitate anything, produce nothing.

– Salvador Dali

Imitation exists everywhere in nature, and we humans are naturally capable of it. Imitating involves observing the original, then reproducing what you find by copying. But what if you're not used to copying anyone? Read on.

If you've never copied another's voice or mannerisms before, you may want to address any fears about doing so before diving in to avoid those fears holding you back.

Some worry they will appear to be mocking an accent, an individual or even an entire group of people. They're fearful of being offensive or caricaturing. This concern looms largest when you start, as the chances are the first attempt won't be perfect.

Where you start with an imitation isn't necessarily where you will end with it. Learning an accent can be like carving a statue from a block of marble. Initially, you may have to take large crude lumps out of the marble to create a rough shape before moving on to the delicate fine detail.

Nevertheless, the perfect copy doesn't exist. The job of the performer is to produce an earnest imitation involving creativity and artistry. After all, when you're onstage you know there is a backstage which isn't seen by the audience. Superman doesn't really fly. You're creating an illusion to allow the audience to suspend their disbelief and engage with the story. So, before you start imitating:

- consider and reaffirm your intention to sincerely connect to the sounds of another's speech, not to mock or deride
- tell yourself that mistakes are an inevitable part of the process (if you haven't already, try the **Have a Bash!** or **Free the Fear** exercises)

Exercise: **Mirror Game**

To develop physical observation skills
You need: a willing person to copy
If you've never imitated a voice before, it may be helpful to imitate movement before sound. This exercise is adapted from the repetition exercise from the Meisner Technique. It's great for training your focus and sharpening your observation skills.

Find a partner and a quiet space with room to move. Your partner is the leader whom you must copy. Face the leader, either standing or sitting. The leader starts creating movements in a slow, steady pattern. Mirror these actions as closely as you can.

The leader frees up the pattern and pace of the movements, doing whatever comes to them. Whatever they do, you follow.

To develop this exercise further: Take it out and about. If your leader is amenable, follow them as they go about a routine task, like walking to the bus stop or making a cup of coffee. Try to get as close as possible to copying every move they make. Focus on each tiny detail – become their carbon copy. The more time you spend noticing and following, the sharper your observational skills will be when it comes to taking on an accent.

Exercise: **Choreo**

To help improve imitation by harnessing intuitive skills
You need: an online dance tutorial, a mirror
Imitation uses the same intuitive skills as a dancer learning choreography. Find an online dance tutorial and choose a style of dance you would feel at least semi-comfortable trying.

Find a space with room to move and play the tutorial. On the first watch, look at the choreographer as you copy. On the second watch, look at yourself in the mirror as you dance. On the third watch, having gained a rough sense of the moves and the flow of the piece, try not to look at anything in particular – just feel what you're doing. The third try is the space in which, having imitated, you start to take ownership of what you're doing to create a performance of what you've found, just as you will do with the accent.

Exercise: **Humalong**

To help gain experience of imitating vocal patterns
You need: a large cushion or pillow
This exercise is useful if you want to practise the overall patterns of a speaker's voice. Put on a podcast or talk radio station using a portable speaker or phone. Get a large cushion or pillow and put it on top of the speaker or phone to muffle the sound. This will mean you're listening to patterns rather than focusing on the words. Set a timer for one minute and copy the patterns of sound you hear using only a hum. Don't try to correct yourself, just hum along to the sound as best as you can.

Do this every day for a week with different podcasts and radio stations. The more you vary what you listen to when practising, the more likely it is you'll be able to pick up the differences in patterns between voices.

Exercise: **Headphone Verbatim**

To help listen in detail, start imitating, reduce self-criticism
You need: an accent recording in audio format, headphones
This way of listening and imitating is drawn from Headphone Verbatim theatre, also called 'recorded delivery', in which actors wear headphones playing the voices of real people from recorded interviews and conversations. In performance, the actors listen and copy the audio with as much precision and accuracy as possible, voicing every word but also 'every inflection, cough, stumble, breath and overlap'.[1]

Put your headphones on and play the accent recording. Check that the volume is at a level where you hear the audio louder than you hear yourself. Close your eyes or lower your gaze and allow the breath to flow.

Play the recording and start repeating what you hear with a delay of about half a second. That way you stay just behind the speaker and keep listening out for what is coming as you speak. Don't worry if you lose track or catch up to them, just breathe and carry on, aiming for that half second delay.

Repeat this several times using the same recording. Resist anticipating or memorizing what is said by keeping to the half second delay so you can stay focused on listening out for every pause, hesitation and change in the detail of the speaker. Let go and let the intuitive right-brain lead, rather than the left-brain which wants to plan!

To develop this exercise further: remove your headphones and find a podcast or a talk radio station. Set a timer for two minutes. During these two minutes, simply repeat as much as possible of what you hear being said from whoever is speaking. This time you will be able to hear yourself, but keep going until the timer runs out, repeating without stopping to correct yourself. The motto here is 'Do it wrong and move along!'

As the podcast or radio continues, set the timer for two minutes again. This time, you may find yourself capturing a sense of the way things are being said. You can try this every day for a week, each day picking a different podcast or radio show to copy. The more you expose yourself to new and varied voices, the better. It'll make the experience more familiar when you learn an accent.

At the end of the week, try a different version of the exercise. Set a timer for five minutes. Pick a podcast or radio programme that you can pause and rewind. Pick something with voices you feel drawn to imitating. Listen and repeat what you hear, capturing a sense of the way things are being said. Whenever you feel like it, pause the recording, rewind and listen again to a small portion to start refining your imitation. Don't agonize about making it perfect, simply listen again and copy more closely. When the time is up, stop working.

Exercise: **Practise, Party! Practise, Party!**

To help make repeat practice manageable and useful and to help hone the new accent

You need: an accent recording, a timer

You may have heard the phrase 'practice makes perfect'. You may even find it in this book! Repeat practice plays a huge role in successful accent work. Honing an accent or one of its features is a bit like forging metal. You have to keep returning it to the fire to work at it again.

But what if you find repetition boring or frustrating? The trick is to make your repeat practice (a) something you actually *do* and (b) mindful, so you stay focused and avoid cementing inaccuracies into your muscle memory.

This exercise helps you to enjoy practising by rewarding yourself with a mini 'party' every time you do it. The structure also keeps the practice time short to stay focused and avoid frustration.

Try this using the steps in the circle below by doing an exercise from the book or your own form of practice. Set a timer for fifteen minutes and start practising.

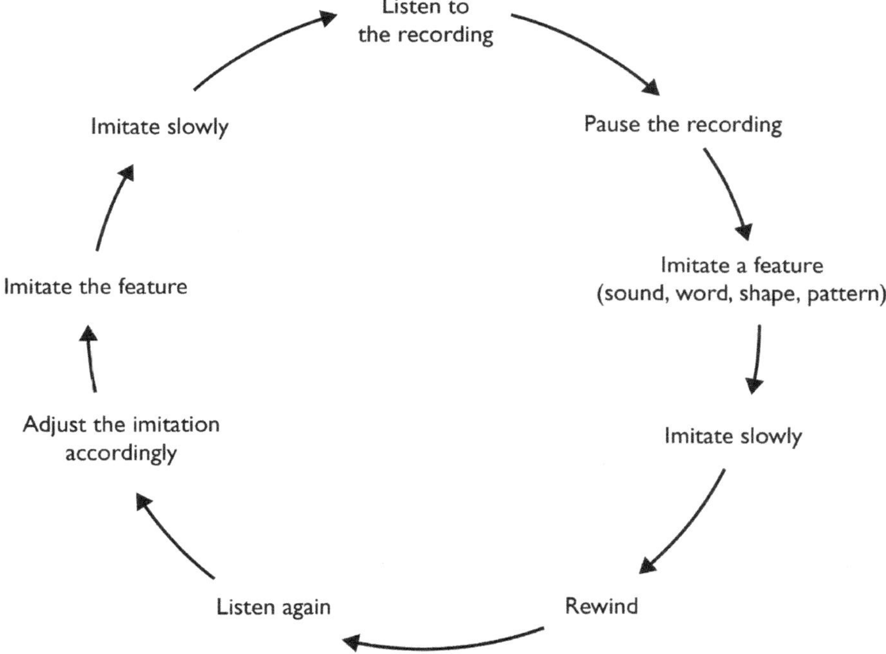

When fifteen minutes is up, stop what you're doing and reward yourself by swapping practice for a five-minute party! You could:

- have a dance party
- sing along to your favourite song
- walk around the block
- sit in a garden
- eat a snack

- read an article
- meditate
- have a nice drink
- stretch
- play a video game
- play with a pet
- doodle
- watch a funny video
- nap

When the five minutes is over, set the timer again and repeat the steps in the circle or your own practice exercise. Carry on alternating using the mantra 'Practise, party! Practise, party!'

Shapes

Shapes refers to the way the articulators **move** and **position** themselves to 'shape' the accent. Shapes are created by the moveable articulators:

- **jaw**
- **lips**
- **tongue**
- **soft palate**

Together, the movements they make most frequently and the positions they return to form the commonly created shapes through which the voice travels.

These shapes also help in creating the **resonant focus** of the accent; the place where the sound is felt to resonate most strongly. Shapes and resonance create an overall quality of sound. The shapes and resonant focus of individual speakers may differ, but there will be certain similarities within an accent group.

Finding the shapes and resonant focus of your chosen accent can be hugely helpful. Sounds may automatically fall into place. Even if you've discovered all the key sounds, finding the shapes through which they all travel might prove vital in tying everything together.

If you'd like to brush up your awareness of the articulators before approaching this, head to **Part A**.

Remember: You can pick and choose which exercises to do. They don't have to be completed in any particular order.

Discovering shapes

Exercise: **For Your Eyes Only**

To help notice the shapes of the lips and jaw through watching
*You need: an accent recording (*video*)*
Watch a video of your speaker with the **sound off**. This way you can really focus on what you see. Focus on their **lips** and ask yourself:

Movements: Are the lips more moving or more still?
Shapes: What shapes do they make most frequently?

Focus on their **jaw** and ask yourself:

Movements: Is the jaw generally more moving or more still?
Positions: Is it more open or closed? Or is it somewhere in the middle?

Write down what you've found in a way that makes sense for you. This could be in note form, in a table or with an image or doodle.

Exercise: **For Your Ears Only**

To help notice the shapes of the accent through listening
You need: an accent recording (audio), headphones
Listen to a recording of the speaker with headphones on. Wearing headphones can help you focus on the sounds. If you have a video recording, don't watch, **just listen** for this exercise.

As you listen, imitate the words and sounds you're hearing as best you can and notice the shapes your articulators are making. Focus on your **lips** as you imitate the accent and ask yourself:

Movements: Are your lips generally more moving or more still?
Shapes: What shapes are they making most frequently?

Focus on your **jaw** as you imitate the accent and ask yourself:

Movements: Is your jaw generally more moving or more still?
Positions: Is it more often open, closed or somewhere in the middle?

Focus on the **tongue** as you imitate the accent and ask yourself:

Movements: Does your tongue feel heavy or light? Is it moving around a lot or is it quite still?
Positions: Where does the tongue tip go to most frequently? Is the back of the tongue body mostly high or low?

Focus on the soft palate as you imitate the accent and ask yourself:

Positions: Does your soft palate feel raised or in a mid-position? If you're unsure, as you're imitating, pinch your nose. If the overall quality changes, this is an indication the soft palate is mid. If it doesn't change much at all, it is probably raised. (If the sound completely stops then the soft palate is lowered but this tends to happen for certain sounds rather than for an overall shape).

Write down anything you've found in a way that makes sense for you.

Exercise: **Polaroids**

To help notice the shapes of the accent
You need: an accent recording (video)
Watch a video of your speaker either with the sound on or off and **pause** it at random intervals. Each time you pause, observe and copy the **lips** and **jaw** positions in the frozen image. Breathe through the shape you've created to feel the space in the mouth. Is it a familiar shape, or is it one you don't usually make?

Play, pause and copy the shapes several times. Are there any shapes that the speaker keeps making, or are they very different each time?

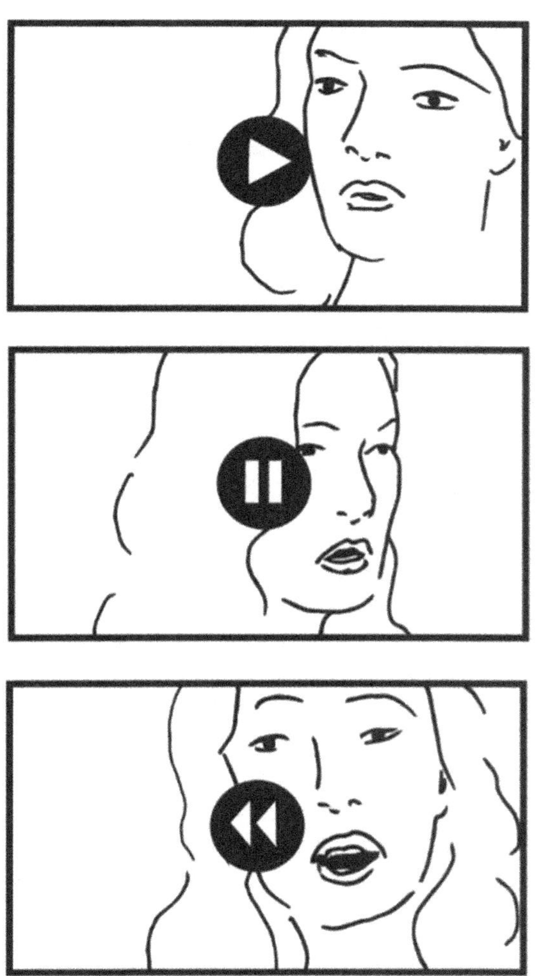

Exercise: **What Are You Thinking?**

To help notice the shapes of the accent
You need: an accent recording (audio or video)
Listen to your recording and focus on any 'ums', 'ers' and 'ahs' your speaker makes. They will usually make these sounds when hesitating or thinking. You may hear a variety of thinking sounds, but there could be one or two that the speaker uses repeatedly.

Choose one sound and copy it as best you can. Lengthen it. Notice the shapes your articulators are making to create it. What are the lips and jaw doing?

Focus on the tongue: Make the sound and with your articulators in this position, breathe in to feel cool air hit the tongue. What shape is it making? Is it high or low in the mouth? Does it feel more forward or more back? Does it feel heavy or light?

Focus on the soft palate: Make the sound again. Is the soft palate raised or in a mid-position? Pinch your nose as you make the sound. If the quality changes, it indicates the soft palate is likely mid. If it doesn't, that indicates that the soft palate is raised.

Write down what you've found in a way that makes sense for you.

Exercise: **Portrait Painting**

To help notice the shapes of the accent
You need: an accent recording (video), something to write with and on
Watch the video of your speaker and draw a picture of them. This image doesn't have to be accurate; it can be as impressionistic as you like. Focus on the lips and the jaw. Draw the shapes you see created most frequently.

Look at your picture. Copy the shapes you've drawn with your own lips and jaw. Do these shapes feel different from your own, or similar?

Exercise: **Puppet Master**

To help explore the shapes of an accent physically
You need: an accent recording
Find a space, and either sit or stand comfortably. Watch and listen to your speaker and focus on their jaw. Is it moving a lot? Is it mostly open, mid or closed? With your hands, represent the positions and movements of the jaw in a way that makes sense to you.

Focus on their lips. Are they moving or still? What shapes are they creating? Let your hands represent the shapes and movements of the lips.

Focus on the tongue tip. Let your arm be the tongue with your fingers as the tongue tip. Where does the tongue tip go most often? Focus on the tongue body. Do you hear a heavy or light tongue? Does it sound generally higher or lower in the mouth? Is it more forward or more back? What animal would this tongue be?

Focus on the soft palate. Let your hands be the soft palate. Do you hear it raised or mid? Move your hands in a way that represents its position.

Doing shapes

Exercise: **Shapeshifting**

To help adopt the shapes of the accent
You need: a mirror

Sit in front of a mirror to observe your articulators. Talk about what you've been doing today. Speak in your own accent and focus on your lips.

As you speak, start to introduce a key lip shape you noticed from the speaker of the accent you're learning. Where appropriate, use this shape frequently. Does that change your sound in any way?

Introduce another lip shape and continue speaking. Build in every key lip shape you noticed. If it makes you want to start doing the accent, go for it!

Focus on the lip movements you noticed. If you didn't see much movement, try to keep your lips still. If you saw a lot, move your lips in this way.

Add in what you noticed about the positions and movements of the jaw. Then focus on the tongue. Did you notice it to be heavy or light? Was there a lot of movement? Was the back of the tongue body generally higher or lower in the mouth than yours? Where was the tongue tip? Add these observations in. Did you notice anything about the soft palate? Did you hear a nasal quality or not? Add any observations in.

Speak through the shapes you've adopted. Do you still sound exactly like you or have your sounds shifted at all? If you aren't already speaking in the accent, give it a go as best you can. Do the shapes help you get closer to your goal?

Exercise: **Slowly Does It**

To help adopt the shapes of the accent
You need: a mirror

Speak some text in the accent as best you can. Add in the lip, tongue, soft palate and jaw shapes you observed. Speak very slowly. Going at a slow pace can help you focus and monitor what you're doing with a greater level of accuracy. If it helps, exaggerate the positions and movements to further experience these shapes.

Once you've found the positions and movements, gradually speed up and reduce the exaggeration. How does this feel? How do you sound?

Exercise: **Polaroids 2**

To help adopt the shapes of the accent
You need: a video of your speaker, some text

Just as in **Polaroids**, play a video of your speaker and pause it randomly. Copy the positions of the lips and jaw you see. Breathe through this mouth shape and speak the text through it. If this makes you want to try the accent, go for it!

Press play again and then pause. Copy this new shape, breathe and speak through it. Repeat this several times, pausing the video, finding the shape, breathing and speaking through it. Remind yourself of the shapes you made. Move from one to the next, as if creating a series of Polaroids. Track the movements of your articulators as you do so.

Speak your text again in the accent, and where appropriate, use these shapes. Do they help to create the overall quality of the accent?

Exercise: **Thinking, Thinking**

To help adopt the shapes of the accent
You need: some text

First, do the exercise **What Are You Thinking?** (p. 50) to help find the 'thinking sounds' of the accent. Choose the one you heard most and imitate it. Lengthen it and focus on what your articulators are doing to create it.

Now, read your text in the accent as best you can, and add in the thinking sound every few words. Let the position of the articulators for the thinking sound dominate the text and influence how the words are pronounced.

Read the text again, this time without the thinking sound. If you find the accent straying, make the thinking sound again to help you find the home base of the articulators.

Resonant focus

When we speak, sound waves bounce around all available space in the vocal tract.

The resonant focus of an accent is where the sound is felt to bounce around, or resonate, most strongly.

It might help to think of this as where you feel the main 'buzz' of your voice. Just like someone may hang out in their living room or the kitchen a lot, the resonant focus is where the accent 'sits', 'lives' or spends most of its time. As you can see in Figure 11, different focal points can include:

- the nasal cavity (nose)
- the pharynx (throat)
- the oral cavity (mouth)
- the lips and teeth

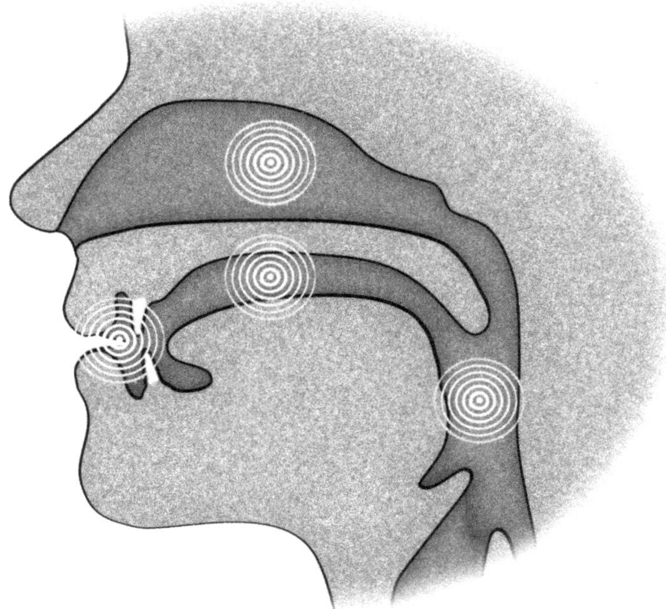

Figure 11 Resonant focal points.

Discovering resonant focus

Exercise: **Spread the Honey**

To help feel the buzz in different resonant areas
Imagine you have some delicious honey. Coat it onto your teeth and lips. Taste it there and express how delicious it is through a 'mmmmmm'. Feel the vibrations on your lips. Imagine that the honey is stuck to the roof of your mouth. Use your tongue tip to scrape it off as you express how delicious it is. Feel the vibrations between the tongue and your hard palate.

Now imagine that you're gargling the honey. Tilt your head back slightly and express how delicious it is with a 'mmm' and then an 'aaah'. Feel the sound in the pharynx (throat). As you're eating the honey, you have an itchy nose. Place the 'mmm' in your nose, and let it turn into a 'nnnnnn'.

Try the exercise again, this time looking at the different areas on the resonant focus image in Figure 11 as you spread the honey around.

Exercise: **The Drone**

To help explore different resonant areas
Imagine you have a little drone that makes a small, buzzing sound. Start a hum on a comfortable note to represent this. You're going to fly this little drone inside your vocal tract and explore the different resonating spaces.

Fly your drone through a nostril into your nasal cavity. As you do this, focus the hum into your nose. You can check whether you've done this by gently pinching your nose. If the sound stops, you're in the nose!

Keep the hum going in your nose, but now play with changing the pitch. Slide up and down to explore different notes. Say the days of the week while continuing to focus the sound into your nose. Does this feel familiar or new to you?

Fly the drone into your pharynx (throat) and repeat the steps. Hum on one pitch and focus the sound there. Then change the pitch, sliding up and down, and say the days of the week in that area. Can you hear a difference from when you were in the nose? Does this feel familiar or new to you?

Fly your little drone into the middle of your mouth, the oral cavity, and direct the hum towards your hard palate (the roof of your mouth). Explore different pitches while focusing the hum here. Say the days of the week. Does this feel familiar or new to you?

Fly your drone to the very front of your mouth, towards your lips and teeth. Explore different pitches while focusing the hum here. Say the days of the week. Does this feel familiar or new to you?

Spend some time flying your drone around these different areas and speaking from each one to notice how your sound quality changes.

Doing resonant focus

Exercise: **Speaker, Speaker, Where Do You Resonate?**

To help notice the resonant focus of your speaker
You need: an accent recording, some text
Listen to the accent recording. When you feel comfortable, start imitating the speaker. Don't worry if you don't manage to say everything they're saying, just keep listening and try your best to copy what you hear. Focus less on the words and more on the quality of the sound. You can even mumble.

Once you have a sense of their sound quality, turn your copying into a hum that matches this quality. Close your eyes and notice where you feel the buzz of the hum most strongly. Is it in the nose, the mouth or further back in the throat?

Speak some text in the accent as best you can and focus the sound into the area you discovered. Have you found the quality of the accent? If it doesn't sound quite right, repeat the exercise and shift the resonant focus to another area. Speak some text using this resonant focus. Does it have a similar quality to the accent?

Exercise: **Return of the Drone**

To help explore the resonant focus of the accent
You need: an accent recording, a text to practise with
Just as in **The Drone**, imagine you have a tiny drone that you fly into your vocal tract. Fly your drone into a particular area and hum into that place. Play the recording. Does

this resonant focus match the general sound the speaker is making? If not, send the drone into different areas until you get as close to your speaker's sound as possible.

Take a line of text and hum it, staying with the resonant focus you found. Speak the text, still focusing the buzz of vibrations into the same area. If you feel able to speak in the accent, go for it.

Take more text. If you find that you're leaving that area of focus at any point, go back to the drone and hum.

Exercise: **Which Way?**

To discover and do the direction of the accent
You need: an accent recording, something to write with and on, some text
In addition to the shapes and the resonant focus of an accent, you may feel the sound is travelling in a particular direction. While it's true that for many individual sounds the air travels out of the mouth, thinking of the overall sound moving in a certain direction can help to find the quality. Directions might include:

- flying out of the mouth like a dart
- falling back into the pharynx (throat)
- flowing through the nose
- bouncing around the soft palate

Play the recording. As you listen, place your pen on the page and draw the journey of the sound, whatever that means to you. This can be as impressionistic as you like. Look at your marks on the page. Can you decipher a general direction from them?

Play the recording again, this time using your hand to track the journey of the sound. What movements are you making? Is your hand moving forward, are you pulling it back, is it spinning or darting? Let your drawings and your movements indicate a possible direction for the accent.

Speak the text in your own accent and picture the sound travelling in this direction. Does it change your sound? Speak the text in the accent as best you can, continuing to picture the sound travelling in this direction. Does this help to find the accent quality?

Patterns

Just as patterns can be found in art, nature and music, they can also be found in accents.

Have you ever found yourself describing an accent as 'choppy' or 'staccato', for instance? Perhaps you've heard someone ending their sentences with the same rise in pitch. Maybe you've noticed speakers of an accent emphasizing words by making them louder.

These are examples of rhythmic, pitch and stress patterns. Recognizing and imitating them can help you to find the flow and increase credibility in an accent.

'Prosody', 'musicality' and 'intonation' are among many terms used to label this accent feature. We chose 'patterns', but it may not work for you. If you prefer another word, we wholeheartedly encourage using that instead. This section:

- defines and describes different types of patterns
- provides exercises to help explore these patterns
- helps you discover and do the patterns of the accent you're learning

Remember: You can pick and choose which exercises to do. They don't have to be completed in any particular order.

Types of patterns

Stress: The way syllables are emphasized.
Rhythm: The interplay between stressed and unstressed syllables.
Pitch: Repeated sequences of notes or recurring melodies.

It may help to think of stress, rhythm and pitch like this: You're on the dance floor and your favourite song comes on. You start by tapping your foot to the main beat. Here, you're feeling the **stress**. The strong beats of the music.

You start to feel this pulse travelling into your body. Your body knows where the strong beats are, but it doesn't just follow these, it enjoys the off beats too. It's dancing to the **rhythm**. The patterns created by the combination of strong and weak beats.

You sing along. Your voice follows the song's melody. You do this by changing **pitch**. Within the song, certain sequences of notes repeat, making this song different from all the others. When patterns of stress, rhythm and pitch come together, they create the music of a particular accent.

You may prefer to focus on stress, rhythm and pitch individually when learning an accent. Alternatively, you might find that one illuminates another, or that it's easier for you to consider all three elements simultaneously. Find out what works for you. If you're unsure where to begin, the exercises **Move to the Music** and **Draw the Patterns** are good places to start.

Exercise: **Move to the Music**

To help notice patterns
You need: an accent recording of conversational speech
Either seated or standing, and with enough room to move, play the recording. As you listen, allow the accent to enter your body. Let the speech patterns affect and guide your movements. You can move your whole body or just a body part.

Notice your movements and the way they make you feel. Are they flowing or jerky? Is your pace fast or slow? Are your actions big and sweeping, or are they small and contained? Are your movements repetitive or is each one unique? How are they affecting your breath and your thoughts?

Do these movements tell you anything about the patterns of the accent? If you're curious about the way your body moved, start with **Rhythmic patterns** on p. 64. If you noticed your body feeling the stronger beats, start with **Stress patterns** on p. 58 and if you were more focused on the melody of the accent, start with **Pitch patterns** on p. 70.

Exercise: **Draw the Patterns**

To help start noticing patterns
You need: an accent recording of conversational speech, something to write with and on
Place your pen on the paper and as you listen to the recording, start to make marks on the page. Don't think too hard about it, let the patterns of speech guide your hand. Do this for at least a minute to give yourself time to notice what you're listening to.

Look at the page. What have you drawn? Shapes? Patterns? Images? Is anything repeated or is it all entirely random? Are any particular patterns jumping out at you?

Do your doodles tell you anything about the patterns of the accent? If your shapes appear to follow the melody of the accent, start with **Pitch patterns** on p. 70. If you see strong beats notated then start with **Stress patterns** on p. 58 and if you've made marks that imply a sense of underlying movement, start with **Rhythmic patterns** on p. 64.

Stress patterns

Stress refers to the way syllables are emphasized or stand out.

Speech Bubble

A syllable is a **beat**.

Some words are made up of only one beat (wolf, sheep, duck) while others are made up of more than one (tiger, elephant, armadillo).

Usually, the number of syllables depends on the number of vowel sounds in a word:

'D**U**CK' has one vowel sound, so it has one syllable.

'**E**L**E**PH**A**NT' has three vowel sounds, so it has three syllables.

Exercise: **Count the Beats**

To help explore the number of syllables in words
Say the following words in your own accent. Clap when you say each syllable:

Egg
Turnip
Tomato
Avocado

It's likely that you will have clapped once for 'egg', twice for 'turnip', three times for 'tomato', and four times for 'avocado'. Some speakers may add more syllables, or use fewer, but these words generally have the same number of syllables regardless of accent.

Exercise: **Beat It!**

To help explore changing the number of syllables in words
You need: recording 2 (https://www.bloomsburyonlineresources.com/the-accent-handbook), an accent recording (reading Ghost Ship, if possible).
Different accents use different numbers of syllables for certain words. Say the following words in your own accent. As you say each one, count the number of syllables you give it by clapping the beats:

Different
Interested
Personally
Solitary
Trembling

Listen to recording 2, which is of two different speakers saying these words. The first speaker gives each vowel sound a syllable, whereas the second reduces the number of possible syllables. This is called **compression** and is a common feature in lots of accents of English.

If you have a recording of your speaker reading *Ghost Ship*, listen to how they say the words in the list. Count the number of syllables your speaker gives each word. Are they using the same, more or fewer than you? Are there any other words in the text that your speaker gives a different number of syllables to? If so, jot them down.

If you don't have a recording of *Ghost Ship*, listen to the recording you do have and note down any words where your speaker uses a different number of syllables to you. Look at your list. Is there a spelling pattern emerging among the words? Do they end with similar letters, for instance? Do the same combinations of letters reappear? Look out for any clues that may help you when applying the accent to text.

Discovering stress patterns

Word stress

Word stress refers to the part/s of a word that are stressed.

Exercise: **Stress Ball**

To help explore word stress within the accent
You need: an accent recording of conversational speech, a bouncy ball
This exercise helps you notice whether the accent stresses words differently to you. The accent could stress a different syllable, or stress more or fewer syllables.

To explore word stress, say the word **vaccine** a few times in your own accent. It's made up of two syllables, 'vac' and 'cine'. Which syllable do you give the stronger beat to?

- Do you place the stress on the first syllable? **vac**cine
- Or do you place it on the second syllable? vac**cine**
- Or perhaps you give both syllables equal stress? **vac cine**

If you're unsure, take your bouncy ball and as you say the word, throw it to the ground. Notice if you throw the ball on a particular syllable. This is likely to be the one you stress. Take the bouncy ball and throw it to the ground on different syllables:

- Throw it down as you say '**vac**' and allow it to bounce back up on 'cine'.
- Throw it down as you say '**cine**'.
- Bounce it on '**vac**' and '**cine**'.

Allow the action of throwing the ball to help you emphasize the syllable/s.

Repeat the exercise with the following words, saying them first in your own accent and then changing the word stress. Use the ball to help you:

Adult

Address

Garage

Advertisement

Play your accent recording. Does the speaker stress every word they say in the same way as you? If not, make a note of words that differ and use the ball to help you practise the word stress. Try improvising in the accent as best you can, using these words. Speak about your favourite book or film, for instance.

Sentence stress

Sentence stress refers to the emphasized words in a sentence. Speakers of English as a first language tend to stress the words in a sentence that carry the most information. What is deemed important information at that moment will depend on the situation. Sentence stress depends on **intention**.

Exercise: **No Stress Robot**

To help explore sentence stress
You need: something to write with and on, a highlighter
Write down the phrase: *I went to the shop to buy an ice cream.*

Say the phrase in your best robot impression. To achieve this, it's likely you aren't making any words or syllables more or less prominent. You're giving everything equal stress.

Say it again but this time as you would in your everyday speech. Which words did you stress? If you're unsure, say the phrase again. Highlight the words you've made more prominent. There is no wrong here, whatever you decided to stress in that moment was correct for your intention.

Try highlighting different words in the sentence and stressing them instead. Does this change the intention of the phrase? Repeat until you've tried stressing the sentence in every possible way.

Ways to stress

Stressing syllables in words and words in sentences can be done in a variety of different ways, using:

- pitch
- volume

- length
- articulation
- pause

Most speakers use a combination of these to communicate, but it can be helpful to notice whether a speaker of an accent uses one more frequently or to a greater or lesser degree than you might.

Tendencies can be heard in speakers of the same accent group, so listening out for how your speaker uses stress can give you important clues to the patterns of the accent.

Exercise: **Stress Swap**

To help explore different ways to stress
You need: a recording device
This exercise can be useful if you want to explore different ways to stress. It's also helpful to free up your habitual stress use. Take the phrase 'I went to the shop to buy an ice cream'. Record yourself saying the phrase and for the purposes of this exercise, stress the following words:

I WENT to the SHOP to buy an ICE cream.

Keep the recording for the end of the exercise. Now, say the sentence five more times and each time, stress the same words but try the following:

- Use ONLY **pitch** (raise or lower the pitch to stress the words).
- Use ONLY **volume** (increase or decrease the volume to stress the words).
- Use ONLY **length** (lengthen or shorten sounds to stress the words).
- Use ONLY **articulation** (increase the consonant energy to stress the words).
- Use ONLY **pause** (pause slightly before the stressed words).

Listen to the recording you made at the start of the exercise. What are you using to stress these words? Are you using one way, or are you using a combination of two or three ways to emphasize the words?

Exercise: **Stress Detector**

To help explore the accent's stress patterns
You need: an accent recording of conversational speech
Listen to the recording. Follow the patterns of stress with your hand so when a word is stressed, you allow your hand to move in response. Where is the speaker placing their strong beats? At the beginning, middle or end of phrases? Or is there no obvious pattern?

Try improvising in the accent as best you can, placing stress in the same places in phrases as the speaker did. Talk about your favourite childhood memory, for instance.

Repeat the exercise, this time noticing the way words are stressed. Use your hand to help you. If you hear an increase in volume, you could raise your hand. If you hear length being used, you could slow your movement down and so on.

What modes of stress does your speaker use the most? Pitch? Volume? Length? Articulation? Pause? Are there any that the speaker isn't using?

Try improvising in the accent as best you can, using the mode/s of stress you noticed to emphasize the words. Remember, the accent is a work in progress so don't worry if it doesn't sound accurate, focus simply on adding the stresses you noticed.

Exercise: **Verbatim Stress**

To help explore stress in the accent
You need: an accent recording of conversational speech, headphones, a recording device
For this exercise you'll need to play your accent recording through headphones. Put your headphones in or on, press play on your recording device to record yourself, and press play on your accent recording. Speak along with it, imitating what you hear as best you can. If you need some verbatim guidance, head to p. 44.

Listen back to the recording of your voice. How are you highlighting keywords in the sentence? If you've used something you don't usually, this is a clue to the speaker's means of stress.

Try improvising in the accent as best you can, using the mode/s of stress you noticed to emphasize words. Talk about your favourite childhood memory, for instance.

Doing stress patterns

Exercise: **Stress Jump**

To help practise the accent's stress patterns
You need: some text, a highlighter
Read your text through in the accent as best you can. Decide which words to stress for the purposes of this exercise and highlight them.

Stand up and read the text again. Every time you get to a highlighted word, jump to mark the stress. Make sure your jumps are on the stressed parts of the words.

Repeat the exercise and use whatever you've noticed your speaker using to stress (pitch, volume, length, articulation, pause) to make the words stand out. If you've noticed more than one way, layer your practice. Start by using one, and then repeat the exercise adding the second and so on. Keep jumping as you do so.

Exaggerate what you're doing to really embed these modes of stress. Once they're embedded, gradually reduce the exaggeration.

Exercise: **Stress Conductor**

To help practise the accent's stress patterns
You need: some text, something to 'conduct' with (real or imaginary)
Read your text in the accent as best you can. Highlight the words to stress for the purposes of this exercise.

Speak your text in the accent again. As you do, conduct yourself as if you were conducting an orchestra. When you get to a stressed word, use a physical gesture to encourage yourself to stress in the way your speaker would.

If you're using pitch, raising or lowering your baton could indicate higher or lower notes, for instance. If you're using volume, opening your arms could indicate louder sounds, or bringing your arms together could encourage quieter sounds. If you're using length, using a gesture to draw out the sounds could help elongate them. If you're using articulation, making short, sharp gestures could indicate sound energy. If you're using pause, find moments of suspension before the stressed words.

Put your baton down and read the text again, this time without gestures, allowing the prior conducting to influence the way you stress the words.

Exercise: **Stress Recorder**

To help practise the accent's stress patterns
You need: some text, something to record with
This exercise can help give you a sense of whether you're matching the stress patterns of the accent. Record yourself reading the text in the accent as best you can. Focus on using the ways of stressing that you've already found in your speaker.

Listen to the recording back. Have you achieved your goal? If you're unsure, listen again to your speaker and compare your ways of stressing with theirs. Have you missed a vital ingredient? If you aren't satisfied with your imitation, record yourself again and then compare recordings.

It can take time to take on someone else's stress patterns so keep practising until it's embedded.

Rhythmic patterns

Rhythm is the interplay between stressed and unstressed syllables. Where stress considers the strong beats and how they're emphasized, rhythm examines both the stressed and unstressed beats and any recurring patterns between them.

Different accents have different rhythmic patterns. For instance, some speakers use choppy, spiky rhythms, while others use smoother, more gliding rhythms. Freeing up your own rhythms and adopting new ones can really help you find the underlying music of the accent you're learning.

Discovering rhythmic patterns

Exercise: **Rhythm Soup**

To help explore different rhythmic possibilities
You need: some text, an accent recording containing conversational speech
This exercise is helpful if you're not used to changing the rhythm of your speech, or you are finding it challenging to shift from your habitual rhythmic patterns.

Stand with some room to move and imagine you're making soup as you read your text. Start speaking your text in your own accent and pretend to chop an onion. Commit to the action and let it influence the rhythm of your speech. Imagine you're peeling carrots. Let this peeling action influence the rhythm of your speech. Imagine you're frying the carrots and onions in a pan. Let the action of pushing the vegetables around the pan influence your rhythm. Imagine you're stirring the thick, blended soup and allow this action to influence your speech. Take time to explore these different rhythmic possibilities, and any others that come to mind. Notice if and how they affect your speech.

Listen to the accent recording and try to match the speaker's rhythm with any of the cooking rhythms you've explored. For example, does the accent feel more like chopping, peeling, pouring or something else?

Jot down anything you noticed that could be useful for the accent you're learning and then improvise in the accent as best you can, incorporating the rhythms you've noticed. Speak about your favourite food, for instance. If it helps, use the physical gestures to help embody the rhythms.

Exercise: **Ballroom Dancing**

To help explore the accent's rhythmic patterns
You need: some text, an accent recording containing conversational speech
This exercise is helpful for freeing up and finding the rhythms of the accent, using a sense of music and movement.

Find a space with some room to move and listen to your accent recording. As you listen, start to move to the rhythms of their speech. Let the recording lead your movements rather than trying to predict the rhythms. Do this for some time to allow yourself to focus on moving to the music.

If you had to compare the way you're moving to a type of dance, which dance would you choose? Are your movements more like the smooth sweeps of a waltz, or are they mirroring the lively bouncing of a jive? Do you feel the rhythms of a heavy hip-hop track or a light and lyrical folk song?

Pause the recording but keep moving in the same way. Speak your text in the accent as best you can and allow your movements to guide the rhythms of your speech.

Read your text again, this time without moving. Allow the prior movements to influence your speech. Note down any discoveries.

Exercise: **Verbatim Rhythm**

To help explore the accent's rhythmic patterns
You need: an accent recording containing conversational speech, headphones, recording device
For this exercise you'll need to play your accent recording through headphones. Put your headphones in or on, press play on your recording device to record yourself, and press play on your accent recording. Speak along with it, imitating what you hear as best you can. If you need some verbatim guidance, head to p. 44.

Listen back to the recording of you speaking. How do you sound? Have you adopted any particular rhythmic patterns that are different from your own? Are you choppier, or smoother? If you've found something different, this is a clue to the accent's rhythm. Try improvising in the accent as best you can, using the rhythmic patterns you discovered.

Doing rhythmic patterns

Exercise: **Feel the Rhythm**

To help practise the accent's rhythmic patterns
You need: some text, something to write with and on
Remind yourself of the rhythms you noticed in the accent. Clap the rhythm as best you can. If clapping doesn't help you, stamp it, sing it or move in a way that imitates it.

Speak your text while clapping/stamping/singing/moving and do your best to make the text fit. It may sound strange, but that's OK. This is to help you break out of your own rhythmic pattern.

Speak your text, keeping the rhythm but leaving the clapping/stamping/singing/moving aside. Does this sound like your speaker? If it sounds too regimented, try dialling the strength of the rhythm down so that you only have hints of it in your speech. Do so until you feel it matches the rhythm of your speaker more closely.

Exercise: **Rhythm Conductor**

To help practise the accent's rhythmic patterns
You need: some text, something to 'conduct' with (real or imaginary)
Imagine you're a conductor. Stand, or sit with your conductor's baton in one hand. Remind yourself of the rhythms you noticed in the accent and start to move your baton in this way.

If you noticed jagged rhythms, imagine a piece of music with these rhythms and move your hands in a concise and staccato way. If you noticed sweeping rhythms, imagine a piece of music with these rhythms and move your hands in a steady, gliding way. If you noticed erratic rhythms with no regularly repeated patterns, imagine a piece of music with these rhythms and move your hands in a more random way.

Still conducting, speak your text in the accent and allow the rhythms to influence your speech. Speak the text again without conducting, but allow your prior actions to influence your speech.

Do these new rhythms affect your breathing or thought processes in any way? Note down anything you consider useful for the accent you're learning, or the character you're playing.

Exercise: **Walk the Rhythm**

To help practise the accent's rhythmic patterns
You need: some text, some space to move
Walk around your space, matching the rhythms you've noticed. If you noticed a steady, regular rhythm, walk in this way. If you notice a jagged, staccato rhythm, move in this way. Does your speaker pause? If so, pause your movements momentarily.

Speak your text in the accent as you walk. Try to match the rhythm of your speech with the way you're moving. As you do this, notice how these rhythms affect your breathing and your thought processes. Note down anything that you think could be useful for the accent you're learning, or the character you're playing.

Stand still and speak the text in the accent. Allow the work you've done to influence the rhythm of your speech.

Language Bubble

If you're learning an accent where English isn't the first language, it can be useful to consider which category of language timing it falls into. Some linguists split languages into three categories:

- syllable-timed
- mora-timed
- stress-timed

If the language is **syllable-timed** or **mora-timed**, the rhythmic pattern will differ from English. Depending on the level of your speaker's English, the rhythmic patterns of their first language may be heard in their spoken English. Exploring and adopting these patterns can be very useful for the accent.

Syllable-timed:
Each syllable lasts roughly the same amount of time, whether it's stressed or not. If you add more words to a phrase, the phrase takes longer to say. Examples of syllable-timed languages: Italian, French, Spanish, Turkish, Cantonese and Mandarin.

Play recording 3: Italian (https://www.bloomsburyonlineresources.com/the-accent-handbook).

Listen to the individual syllables of the Italian language. Don't worry if you cannot understand, this can actually make listening for syllables easier. Can you hear that they're given roughly equal time? It may help to move to the beats.

Listen to the same speaker speaking English. Notice how the same rhythms have transferred into English so that each syllable is given a similar length.

Mora-timed:
Languages use mora, not syllables. Mora are very short syllables and the duration of each of these is equal. Examples of mora-timed languages: Japanese, Ganda, Slovak and Gibraltese.

Play recording 4: Japanese (https://www.bloomsburyonlineresources.com/the-accent-handbook).

Listen to the individual mora of the Japanese language. Don't worry if you cannot understand, this can actually make listening for mora easier. Can you hear that each beat is equal? It may help to move to the mora. Listen to the same speaker speaking English. Notice how the same rhythms have transferred into English so that each syllable is given equal weight and time.

Stress-timed:
Syllables do not last the same amount of time, but the interval between two stressed syllables is equal. Adding more words to a sentence will not necessarily make it longer. Instead, unstressed syllables are shortened to fit between the stressed syllables. Examples of stress-timed languages: English, German, Dutch, Danish, Persian and Thai.

Play recording 5: German (https://www.bloomsburyonlineresources.com/the-accent-handbook).

The speaker is speaking German. Listen to the individual syllables of the language. Don't worry if you cannot understand, this can actually make listening for syllables easier. Can you hear that the syllables vary in length?

Listen to the same speaker speaking English. Notice how some syllables are short and some are longer. Notice how the same rhythms have transferred into English.

Exercise: **Rhythmic Roots**

To help find the rhythmic base of second language accents
You need: a recording of the first language of your speaker, an accent recording in English, some text

If you have a recording of your speaker talking in their first language, listen to it. If you don't, find a recording of someone speaking that language.

Listen to the recording. Move your body to the rhythms of the language. For example, you could allow it to influence the way you walk around the room, or you could move a body part along with the rhythms. Spend some time listening to the language to immerse yourself in it.

Read your text in English while moving as you were. Allow the movements to influence the rhythm of your speech.

Listen to a recording of your speaker talking in English. Continue to move in the same way. Can you hear the same rhythmic patterns? Are they as strong, or are they weaker? Perhaps they aren't there at all? Do you need to adjust your movements to help fit the rhythms of the speaker's English?

Read your text in the accent. If you've adjusted your movements from the first language to English, move in this new way as you speak. If you haven't made any shifts, move as you were when listening to the first language. Let the movements affect your speech.

Read your text again, this time without any movements. Allow the discoveries you've made to influence the rhythms of your speech.

Exercise: **Weak or Strong?**

To explore the strong and weak forms in an accent
You need: a recording device, an accent recording, some text

English is a stress-timed language (see 'Language Bubble' on p. 66), meaning unstressed syllables are shortened to fit between the stressed syllables. What does that sound like? Certain words can sound smaller or reduced and the vowel sounds can change. This happens in many accents of English as a first language. In syllable-timed or mora-timed languages, syllables are given roughly the same amount of time. When speakers of these languages speak English, often they tend to form each word more fully.

Read the following two phrases in your own accent:

It's them and us.
Let's go and visit them.

Consider how you say the word 'them' in both phrases. Do you say the word in the same way both times 'thEm'? Or do you shorten 'them' in the second phrase to more of a 'thm'? If you do, you are using a weak form of the word in this instance.

Find a comfortable position. Press record on your device and, in your own accent, talk about your weekend plans. Imagine you're speaking to a friend rather than into a voice recorder.

Listen to your recording. Focus especially on the 'little' words you say: a, an, the, in, on, to, him, her and so on. Do you always use the strong forms of these words (saying them fully), or do you use the weak forms too (shortening them and changing the vowel)?

If you and your speaker do the same thing, apply that to your text. If you notice that your speaker uses more weak forms than you:

Underline the important words in each phrase of your text. This will depend on the intention of the line, but usually verbs, nouns and adjectives are emphasized over the 'little' words. Imagine you have a pond in front of you, and stepping-stones crossing it. Read the text, and jump to the different stones, landing on these important words. For the 'little' words, make them as small and insignificant as possible. If you need to listen to your speaker again to notice and copy the sounds they made, do so.

If you notice that your speaker uses more strong forms than you, picture a pond in front of you, with stepping-stones crossing it. Read your text, landing on a stepping-stone for every word you say. As you land, emphasize the word in its strong form.

Read your text again, this time standing still. If you are working on adding in more weak forms, focus on reducing and shortening the vowels in these words. If you are working on adding in more strong forms, focus on saying the words in their fullest form.

Pitch patterns

Pitch patterns refers to repeated sequences of notes or recurring melodies in speech.

Babies learn notes before they learn words. They learn to understand and imitate the pitch patterns of phrases used by their caregivers. Have you ever heard a toddler talking gobbledygook that seems to make absolute sense? This could be due to the rising or falling inflections they are using, or the particular interval between notes.

These patterns are ingrained in us early on and become part of the music of our accent. Everyone uses particular patterns to express themselves, and these can often be heard within speakers of the same accent group. Picking out and imitating these pitch patterns can be a very helpful way into the accent you're learning.

Discovering pitch patterns

Exercise: **Pitch Perfect**

To help compare your pitch patterns with the accent's
You need: a recording device, an accent recording of someone speaking passionately
Find a comfortable position. Press record on your device and, in your own accent, talk about what you did yesterday. Include something you enjoyed about the day and something you didn't. Imagine you're speaking to a friend rather than into a voice recorder.

Listen back. Try humming along to your pitch patterns, following them as best you can. Do you find yourself using any particular patterns? Maybe you go up or down repeatedly. Or perhaps you tend to finish sentences in the same way each time. Do you use very few notes, or a large range?

Repeat the exercise, but this time talk about something you feel passionately about. This could be anything, as long as it excites you.

Listen to your second recording and hum along. Have you used any particular patterns that differ from the first recording? Are they more exaggerated when you speak passionately?

Listen to the accent recording and repeat the exercise, humming along to the speaker's pitch patterns. Ask yourself the same questions: Do they use many different notes or very few? Do they go up or down repeatedly? Do they tend to finish sentences in the same way? Do you use any of the same pitch patterns as your speaker? Are there any that your speaker uses that you don't which could be useful to imitate?

Noticing what you do can be a useful starting point, especially if your speaker does something contrasting. If this is the case, it's important to let go of your own patterns to make way for the new ones. Note down any discoveries.

Exercise: **Melody Maker**

To help explore and apply different pitch patterns to a line of text
You need: an accent recording containing conversational speech
Take the phrase: *It's a beautiful day today.* Say it in your own accent a few times. Then hum the notes you used, matching the melody as closely as you can.

Hum on one note continuously. Don't change the pitch at all. Try speaking the phrase using only this note. Make it completely monotone.

Hum, starting on one note and gliding down in pitch. Try speaking the phrase matching this pattern by starting on a note and then gradually move down in pitch throughout the phrase. It may sound unusual to you, but this is about freeing up your own habitual pitch patterns.

Start on one note and gradually glide up in pitch on a hum. Try speaking the phrase matching this pattern by starting on a note and then gradually moving up in pitch throughout the phrase.

Try humming a note, gliding down in pitch and then gliding up again. Try speaking the phrase matching this pattern.

Hum a completely random pattern and then use it as you speak the phrase. If you're curious about creating and applying any other patterns, try them.

Listen to the accent recording. Do you notice any of the patterns you were humming being used repeatedly? If so, note them down as pitch patterns to integrate into the accent. Perhaps you noticed other pitch patterns that you did not explore on a hum. If so, practise humming them now and note them down.

Exercise: **Depicting Patterns**

To help notice the accent's pitch patterns
You need: an accent recording of conversational speech, something to write with and on
Listen to the accent recording with pen and paper. As you listen, let your pen follow the pitch patterns of the speaker in line form. If your speaker rises in pitch, let the line go up, and if they fall in pitch, let the line go down.

Every time your speaker starts a new phrase, start a new line. Try to follow the patterns as closely as you can. Look at your drawings. Are there any repeated line patterns? Can you pick out two or three that reoccur the most?

Try imitating these patterns. Start by humming one of them. Then, speak a sentence using this pattern. Try using the same pattern with a different phrase. Repeat the exercise with the next pattern. Improvise in the accent using these patterns. Try to use them in similar ways to the speaker. For example, if you heard the same pattern in every phrase use it often, whereas if you heard it more sporadically, use it more sparingly.

Exercise: **Verbatim Pitch**

To help explore the accent speaker's pitch patterns
You need: an accent recording containing conversational speech, headphones, recording device
Put your headphones on or in, press play on your recording device to record yourself, and press play on your accent recording. Speak along with it, imitating what you hear as best you can. If you need some guidance on verbatim, head to p. 44.

Listen back to the recording of you speaking. How do you sound? Have you adopted any particular pitch patterns that are different from your own? Perhaps you used more or fewer notes than you do habitually? Or maybe you used bigger or smaller jumps between notes? Did your intonation rise, fall or remain on one note? If you've noticed anything different, this could be a clue to the accent's pitch patterns. Try improvising in the accent as best you can, using the pitch patterns you observed.

Exercise: **Playing the Pitch**

To help notice the accent speaker's pitch patterns
You need: an accent recording containing conversational speech, some text
Listen to the recording and choose a phrase with a pitch pattern that interests you.

Listen to it a few times, focusing on the melody. Hum along with it as you listen, imitating it as closely as you can. Do this several times and find a way to note it down so you can remember it.

Listen to the recording again and this time focus on the words. Say the words in the accent as best you can using the melodic pattern you've observed. How similar to your speaker can you make it?

Repeat this exercise with two more phrases. Make sure the phrases have different pitch patterns from the first. Find a way to note them down so you can remember them.

Using the three pitch patterns you noticed, improvise in the accent as best you can. Your speaker probably won't use these same patterns all the time, but if it helps to repeat these patterns when practising the accent, that's fine. Once you've embedded them into the accent, use them more sparingly as you go on to text or into performance.

Doing pitch patterns

Exercise: **Pattern Weaver**

To help practise the accent speaker's pitch patterns
*You need: the patterns from **Depicting Patterns**, some text, something to write with and on*
Look at the patterns you drew in **Depicting Patterns**. Hum each pattern a few times to help memorize it.

Take a line of text and the first pattern. Apply the pitch pattern to the text as best you can. Then repeat with the second pattern. Use the same line of text so that you can hear the different tunes. Repeat with a third pattern.

Look through your text. Would any of these patterns work particularly well with other sentences? If so, draw them either above or to the side of the text to remind yourself. If you're unsure, listen to your recording again and note when the speaker uses these patterns. For example, is it when they're asking questions, or perhaps when they're ending phrases? Any clues will help when you apply the pitch patterns to your text.

Read your text through in the accent as best you can, using the patterns you've drawn. Do these patterns work? If you feel a different pattern would work better for a different phrase, try using that instead.

Exercise: **Name That Song!**

To help explore the accent's pitch patterns (this one is for the musicians!)
You need: an accent recording containing conversational speech, some text
Listen to your speaker and notice if there are any intervals (distance between notes) that stand out to you. This could be a very small interval, for instance, or a big jump between notes.

Hum the interval. Repeat it a few times to become familiar with it. Does this interval remind you of an interval in a song you know? Perhaps it's similar to the two notes at the start of the theme tune from 'Jaws', for instance, or the first interval of the 'Star Wars' theme tune. If a song comes to mind, find it and listen to it. Hum along to find the interval in question.

Sing your text using the interval you observed in the song. First, use the interval for every single word or couple of words you say to really embed it. Listen to the accent recording again and notice how often this interval appears. Speak your text, using the interval as often as it feels appropriate for the accent.

Exercise: **Making Music**

To help put stress, rhythmic and pitch patterns together
You need: some text
Find some space with room to move. Read your text once through in your own accent and notice your own stress, rhythmic and pitch patterns.

Focus on the stress patterns of the accent you are learning. Create a gesture to help describe the stress patterns of your speaker. For example, if you notice that they increase in volume, you could try raising your hand each time they do it.

Read the text through in the accent as best you can, doing the gesture when you want to stress a particular word and allowing the gesture to influence how you speak it.

Focus on the rhythmic patterns you noticed. Find a movement in your body which represents these patterns. Don't use a gesture, find a movement within your torso. If you noticed slow, flowing movements, you could play with a slow sway, for instance. Read the text through in the accent as best you can, doing this movement and allowing it to influence how you speak.

Read the text again, this time incorporating the stress and rhythmic patterns. Complete your gesture on the stressed words and allow the movement in your torso to help you find the rhythm.

Focus on the pitch patterns. Gently hum any patterns you noticed. Read your text in the accent as best you can and follow the pitch patterns you hummed.

Read your text another time, incorporating the gesture for the stress patterns, the movement for the rhythmic patterns and the pitch patterns you hummed.

Read it again, this time letting go of physical movements and gestures and focusing on the text. Allow the work you've done to influence the patterns of your speech.

Sounds

Speech sounds are the individual units of sound that make up syllables and words. Both in spelling and in speech, they're divided into two major categories:

- consonants
- vowels

Sounds in English have more variety than spelling. Take the consonant 'C' in **C**up and sau**C**er. Although the C is used both times in the spelling, those are two different sounds.

Sounds of the accent can be useful to learn if they stand out to you and are different from your own.

Remember: You can pick and choose which exercises to do. They don't have to be completed in any particular order.

Exercise: **Sound Shortlisting**

To help notice key sounds of the accent
You need: an accent recording, something to write with and on, some coloured pens or highlighters (optional)
This exercise can help you prioritize sounds to learn or refine for the accent. You may well find that you don't have to change every sound to take on the new accent. Focusing on a few can help establish some goalposts, save time and avoid overload.

Play the accent recording. Scribble down any words that stand out to you. It could be because they sound different from yours or are simply interesting in some way.

On the second listen, look at the words you've written down. As the recording plays and you hear those words again, circle any parts of the word that stand out as being different or interesting. If you're unsure, pause the recording and replay the word. Imitate it if that helps.

Look at what you've circled. Some letters? A part of the word like the beginning, middle or end? Perhaps you wrote a phrase down because you were curious about the joins between words?

Using what you've circled, make a separate list of those interesting sounds. Note them in any way that makes sense to you. This is your shortlist of sounds to learn.

You can use this list to help you decide which sounds to focus on. Perhaps you'd like to try the R sound first. Go to the R section. Maybe you'd prefer to look at that curious vowel sound. Head to the 'Vowel' section.

What are vowels and consonants?

This section is about how vowels and consonants are made. If you are confident in your understanding of sounds, head straight to **Consonant Sounds** (p. 83) or **Vowel Sounds** (p. 142) to discover and do the accent's sounds.

Consonant sounds are **obstructed**: they're made when two articulators come together, or when one articulator moves to another articulator to obstruct the airflow in some significant way. Consonant sounds can be made with any of the articulators.

Vowel sounds are **unobstructed**: they're made when the articulators move to shape the airflow, but they don't obstruct it. Vowel sounds are made mostly with the tongue body and the lips, although the jaw, soft palate and pharynx can also influence the sound.

It may help to think of it like this: air comes up from the lungs. It passes through the larynx (voice box) and from there upwards, it gets shaped into vowels and chopped into consonants. The sounds closely follow one after another to form words.

Exercise: **Consonant or Vowel?**

To experience the difference between a vowel and a consonant
Start by making a 'V' sound. Lengthen it and notice how and where you're obstructing the airflow. Now move to an 'AH' sound and lengthen it to notice how and where the sound is being made. Move back and forth between 'V' and 'AH' a few times.

You may notice that the 'V' (a consonant sound) is created by making an obstruction which forces the air to escape through a small gap towards the front of the mouth. The 'AH' (a vowel sound) isn't obstructed, the air simply exits through an unobstructed space.

If you're curious, explore some other sounds and notice whether you think an obstruction is being made. Can you start to categorize sounds as either vowels or consonants this way?

How consonants are made

Exercise: **Consonant Twister**

To help experience how various consonant sounds can be made
Consonant sounds can be made with the following articulators:

- two lips
- bottom lip and top front teeth
- tongue tip or blade and top front teeth

- tongue tip or blade and gum ridge
- tongue tip and behind the gum ridge
- tongue tip and hard palate
- front of the tongue body and hard palate
- middle of the tongue body and soft palate
- back of the tongue body and uvula
- tongue root and pharynx
- vocal folds

Similarly to the game 'Twister', allow the bullet points to determine which articulator goes where. Find the pairing and explore making a sound with them.

How many different sounds can you make with those two articulators? Challenge yourself to find at least two different ones. How many of these sounds are ones you make and how many are new? Any new sound could prove useful for a different accent.

Exercise: **Consonant Voicing**

To help experience voiced and voiceless consonant sounds

Consonant sounds are either **voiced** or **voiceless**. To explore the difference, put your fingers gently on the front of your neck and hum. Can you feel the vibrations? That's your vocal folds coming together in the larynx and vibrating to create a **voiced** sound (Figure 12).

Make an 'S' sound, like you're imitating a snake. Lengthen it and put your fingers gently on the front of your neck again. Have the vibrations disappeared? This sound is **voiceless**, meaning the vocal folds are open, and the sound is made with just breath passing through the obstruction (Figure 13).

Say the following consonant sounds in your own accent and lengthen them if possible. Keep your fingers on the front of your neck to feel for any vibrations:

Z, SH, D, N, TH, F, K, H

Which ones did you feel vibration for? Some accents may voice a consonant that you don't, or vice versa, so it is useful to be able to move between voiced and voiceless versions where possible. Make the consonant sounds again. If you are voicing a sound, can you make a voiceless version? (See Figure 14).

Exercise: **Straw Obstruction**

To help experience various types of consonant obstruction
You need: a non-rigid straw (not made of metal or glass)

Various types of obstruction produce various consonants. One way of experiencing this is by using a non-rigid straw to imitate the air flow, and your fingers to imitate the articulator actions. These aren't exact imitations of what is happening, but they may help you explore different types of obstruction. Each obstruction has a name as you'll see below. For a definition of terms, go to the 'Speech Bubble' on p. 79.

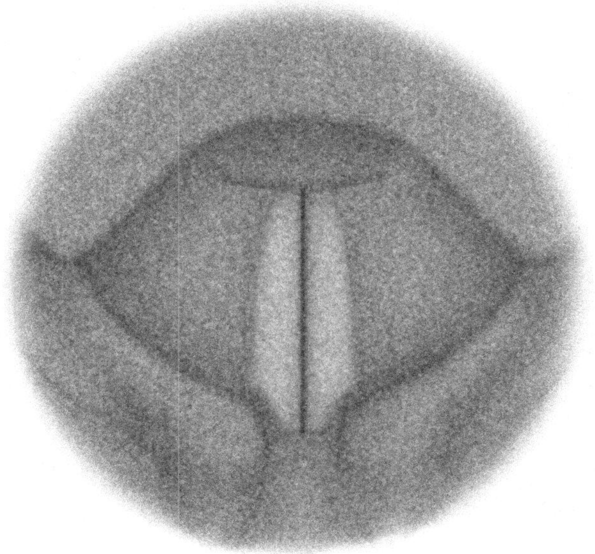

Figure 12 Vocal folds closed.

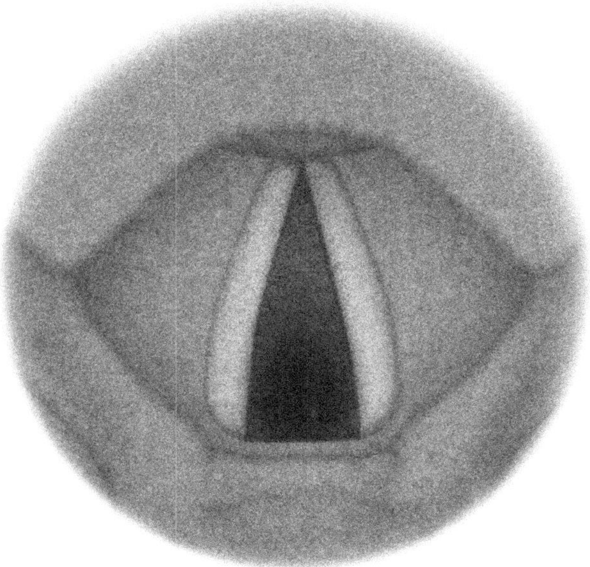

Figure 13 Vocal folds open.

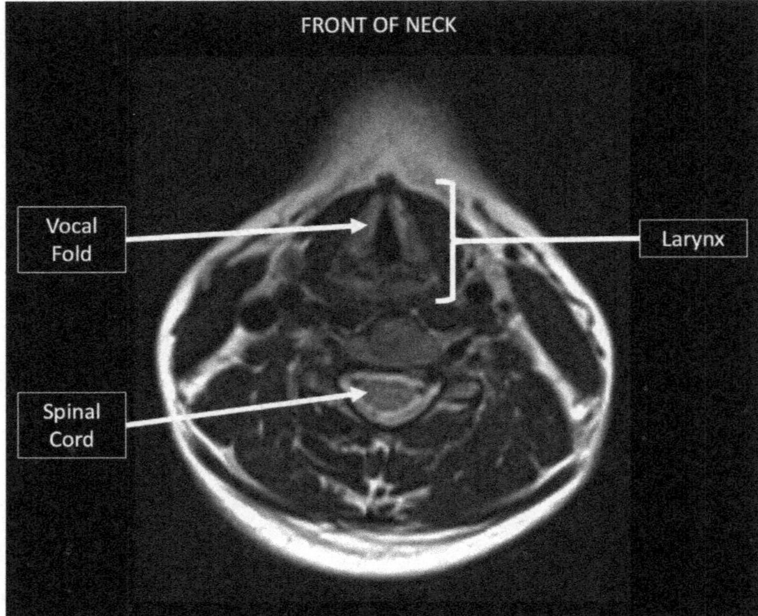

Figure 14 MRI of vocal folds.

Plosive
Place the straw in your mouth and make a sound down it. Pinch the sides together to completely stop the flow of air. Air will build up. Keep trying to make sound and release the sides to create a little explosion. Can you feel the air being released? Place your other hand at the bottom end of the straw to feel the puff of air.

Nasal
Bring the straw under your nose and breathe through it. To voice the sound, make an 'M'. Can you feel the air travelling out of your nose and down the straw? Place your other hand at the bottom end of the straw to feel the airflow.

Tap or flap
Place the straw in your mouth and make a sound down it. Pinch the sides together quickly and immediately release them. This may feel like a plosive. The difference is there was no build-up of air before the release. Place your other hand at the bottom end of the straw to feel a very small puff of air. Can you make this puff of air much less explosive than the plosive?

Trill
Place the straw in your mouth and make a sound down it. Pinch the sides together very quickly and repeatedly to make a series of taps. Place your other hand at the

bottom end of the straw to feel the puffs of air. In reality, a trill is not a series of muscular actions, rather one or more articulators 'fluttering' in the air flow – but that is difficult to achieve with a straw!

Fricative

Place the straw in your mouth and make a sound down it. Bring the sides of the straw very close together so that the flow of air has a 'hissing' quality, but don't let them quite touch. What is the closest together you can go before the flow of air is stopped and you create a plosive?

Approximant

Place the straw in your mouth and make a sound down it. Pinch the sides towards each other so that you're changing the shape of the straw but not enough to create friction. Where is the point at which an approximant becomes a fricative, and a fricative becomes a plosive?

Speech Bubble

Consonant sounds can be classified in three ways:

- **voice**
- **place**
- **manner**

VOICE
Whether the vocal folds come together or stay apart to make the sound.

Voiced: vocal folds come together and vibrate to create sound
Voiceless: vocal folds are apart. Sound is made by breath alone

PLACE
Where in the vocal tract the sound is made.

Bilabial: two lips
Labiodental: bottom lip and top front teeth
Dental: tongue tip or blade and top front teeth
Alveolar: tongue tip or blade and gum ridge
Post-alveolar: tongue tip or blade and just behind gum ridge
Retroflex: tongue tip and hard palate
Palatal: front of the tongue body and hard palate
Velar: middle of the tongue body and soft palate (this may feel like you're engaging the back of the tongue body)
Uvular: back of the tongue body and uvula
Pharyngeal: tongue root and pharynx
Glottal: vocal folds

MANNER

How the articulators come together to obstruct the airflow and make the sound.

Plosive:

Two articulators come together, or one moves to the other to create a closure. Air builds up behind them and air blows them apart.
Pocket Coach: think explosion.

Nasal:

Soft palate lowers to close off the mouth so that air is directed through the nasal passage.
Pocket Coach: think nose.

Tap or flap:

One articulator makes contact with another very briefly. Unlike a plosive, air doesn't build up behind them. For a tap, the moveable articulator starts at point A, moves to point B and then returns to point A. For a flap, the articulator starts at point A and moves to point B. The resulting sound of taps and flaps is the same.

Trill:

Two articulators make contact with one another repeatedly by fluttering in the flow of air.

Fricative:

Two articulators come towards each other, or one moves to the other to create a very narrow passage through which the air passes. Because the space is very small, the air 'hisses' through.
Pocket Coach: think friction.

Approximant:

Two articulators come towards each other, or one moves towards the other to obstruct the air, but they don't touch or come close enough to create friction.
Pocket Coach: think approximately.

Exercise: **Construct a Consonant**

To help explore making different consonant sounds
Consonants can be described in terms of their voice, place and manner. Choose a voice, a place and a manner from the lists in this Speech Bubble and try to create a sound using what you've selected. For example: voiced bilabial plosive – what is the resulting sound?

Change one element of the consonant (either the voice, place or manner) and try making that sound. How different is it from the first? Change another element.

Keep exploring by changing one element at a time. How many different consonants can you make? How many do you recognize as sounds in your own accent? How many are new?

How vowels are made

Exercise: **Tongue Animation**

To help explore tongue movements for vowels
You need: the tongue animation video (Video 1, https://www.bloomsburyonlineres ources.com/the-accent-handbook), a mirror
Vowel sounds are always voiced, meaning the vocal folds come together and vibrate. Vowel sounds are made predominantly with the tongue body and the lips.

To explore how the tongue body helps to create vowels, play the Tongue Animation video. It shows the tongue moving to different positions.

Watch it a few times to familiarize yourself. Pause the video every time the tongue changes position. Copy the position of the tongue as best you can. This may take time and it might help to observe your tongue in the mirror.

Make a sound through the shape. Do you recognize this as a sound in your own accent or something new?

Press play until a different position is shown. Pause the video, copy this position and make a sound through it. Repeat until you've explored every position in the video. Can you recall and recreate the different positions? Make sound through all the positions you can remember.

Exercise: **Lip Logistics**

To help explore various lip shapes for vowels
The lips can move in various ways to shape vowels. Different accents require different lip shapes. To explore this, let your tongue lie in your mouth, doing nothing. Make an AH with your tongue in this position. Keep the sound going, replacing the breath when you run out. As you make the sound, with your tongue doing as little as possible, start to move the lips.

Move them into a pouty shape (Figure 15).

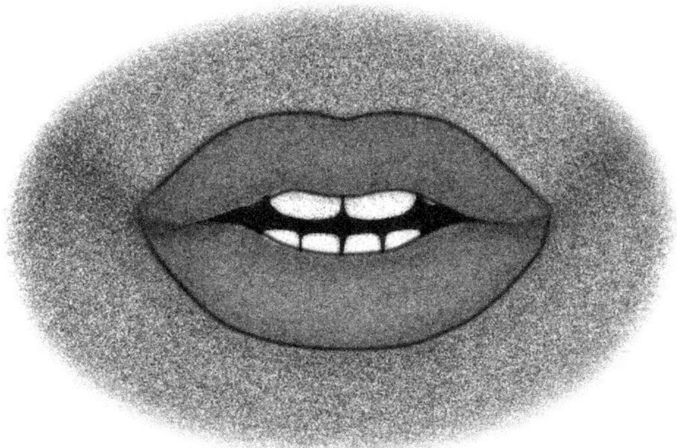

Figure 15 Pouty lips.

Notice if this made a difference to the sound. Move them into a rounded shape (Figure 16). Notice if this made a difference to the sound. Spread them wide (Figure 17). Notice if this made a difference to the sound. Relax the lips so they're doing very little. Did this change the sound?

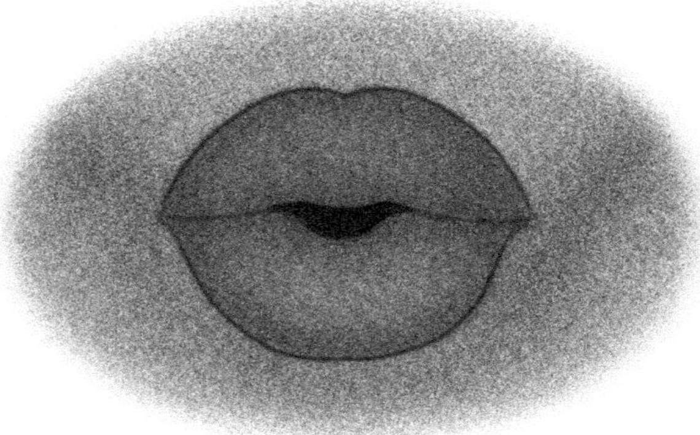

Figure 16 Rounded lips.

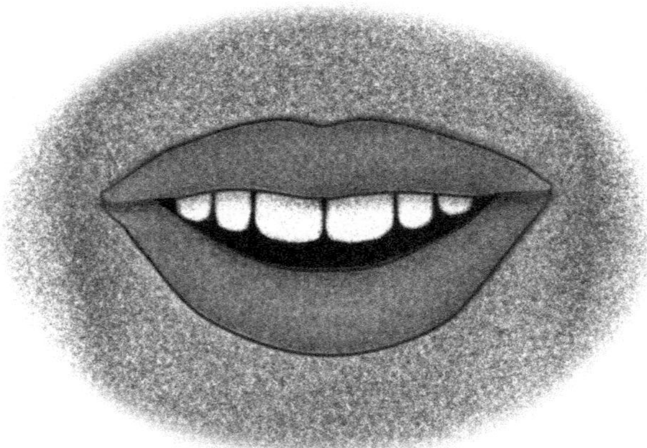

Figure 17 Spread lips.

Move the lips in any way you choose, still with your tongue doing very little. Notice the changes to the sound. As you moved the lips you may have noticed the tongue wanting to move as well. The tongue and lips work together to shape vowel sounds and often they move in unison. Practising moving them separately can be useful for accent work.

Finally, experiment with moving both the tongue and the lips, noticing how different movements and shapes can alter the sound.

Consonant sounds

The following consonant sounds and features tend to vary in accents of English and can therefore be useful to listen out for:

R

L

TH

T

H

NG

Yod

Consonant Clusters

Voicing

Of course, other sounds may jump out at you. Some accents might have an interesting S sound, for example, or a fascinating W sound. In these cases, include them in your exploration too.

Exercise: **Consonant Checklist**

To help narrow down the focus sounds for the accent
You need: an accent recording
The **Sound Shortlisting** exercise (p. 74) can help you work out which vowel and consonant sounds to focus on. **Consonant Checklist** is for consonants only.

Play your accent recording, listening out for these consonants one at a time:

- R
- L
- TH
- T
- H
- NG

A consonant might be key to the accent if it's different from yours. Play the recording and ask yourself:

- Does it sound different to mine?
- Do I hear it being made more or less frequently than mine?
- Do I hear more than one version of the consonant?

If you answer 'yes' to any of these questions, or you're unsure about what you hear, investigate that consonant further using exercises in this consonant section.

Remember: You can pick and choose which exercises to do. They don't have to be completed in any particular order.

R

R can be seen in words as follows:

> Sarah and **R**o**r**y c**r**uised thei**r** ba**r**ge unde**r** a na**rr**ow **r**ed b**r**idge.

The R can be key if the new accent:

- makes the R more or less frequently than you = **R Number**
- pronounces the R differently from you = **R Type**
- has a different range of R Types to you = **R Range**

Discovering R

These exercises are to help work out how the accent pronounces Rs. If you already know what the accent does with Rs, head to the 'Doing R' section for practice.

Exercise: **Feel Your R**

*To gain awareness of your own **R Type**, **R Number** and **R Range***
If you're not sure how and where you make your R sounds, slowly say these words:

> red
> narrow
> bridge

Notice the movements and resistance to the airflow as you form the R sounds. Make a hand movement, describe or draw a shape to remind yourself of what you felt. There is no need to go into detail here. You're simply becoming more aware of your **R Type**.

Some of us make an R sound every time it's written in a word, and some of us don't. If you're not sure what you do, slowly read these words:

> roar
> their
> barge
> under

Slow right down when you come to an R in the spelling. If you feel your articulators coming together or towards each other in some way, you're probably making that R. If you don't feel any distinct movement, you're probably not making that R. How many of the Rs did you make? If you're unsure, deliberately make every R in each word. Does this sound the same as when you say the words in your own accent or not? This can help you gain awareness of your **R Number**.

Read the words once more and whenever you say an R, notice whether you make it in the same way as the previous one. Some of us have only one R Type in

our accent, while some of us have more than one. This can help determine your
R Range.

Exercise: **R Dance**

To help explore the accent's ***R Number***
You need: an accent recording
Get into a position to move, either standing or sitting. Make your R sound by saying
the first sound in the word 'red'. Make up a dance move to accompany the sound.
This could be a movement which reminds you of the sound or it could be abstract.
Do it with your whole body or just a body part. Make it a clear, committed movement.
Repeat the R sound and exaggerate the move. Take it to level 10 commitment! Say
the words 'red', 'narrow' and 'bridge' in your own accent and do the dance move
every time you say the R.

Play the recording. Every time you hear an R being made by the speaker, do
the dance move. Make sure you actually hear it, rather than just expect it. Play the
recording once more and when you hear an R in a word, do the dance move and
allow yourself to gently echo that word as you heard it as best you can.

Are you doing your dance move and echoing the R every time an R is in the
spelling? If so, chances are this accent is **rhotic**. Are you only doing the dance move
sometimes? Chances are this accent is **non-rhotic** or **variable**. To learn what these
terms mean, head to the Speech Bubble on p. 86.

Exercise: **R Hunting**

To help explore the accent's ***R Number***
You need: an accent recording, something to write with and on
Use a recording of *Sarah and Rory cruised their barge under a narrow red bridge* or
pick one phrase from the recording that contains Rs. Write down the sentence or
phrase so you can see the Rs in the words on the page. You could even highlight
them or draw arrows so the Rs stand out for you.

Play the clip several times to familiarize yourself with it. Listen again and look
at the sentence or phrase you've written down. Circle every R sound you hear in
the recording. Be careful not to assume that you hear the R just because it's in the
spelling. Do you actually hear the sound being made, or do you just hear the vowel
sound before it?

If you're unsure, allow yourself to gently echo each word as best you can. As you
copy the words, notice if your articulators are moving to create the R or not. If they
are, circle the R.

If you circled every single R on the page, chances are this accent is **rhotic**. If you
only circled some Rs, but not all of them then chances are this accent is **non-rhotic**
or **R variable**. To learn what these terms mean, head to the Speech Bubble on p. 86.

R Number or 'rhoticity' in accents of English is grouped as follows:

Rhotic:
Pronounce every R that is written.
Pocket Coach: See an R, say an R!
Sa**R**ah and **R**o**R**y c**R**uised thei**R** ba**R**ge
Listen to recording 6 *(https://www.bloomsburyonlineresources.com/the-accent-handbook).*

Non-rhotic:
Pronounce R before vowel sounds but not after them.
*Pocket Coach: R in **crash** but not in **car**!*
Sa**R**ah and **R**o**R**y c**R**uised their barge
Listen to recording 7 *(https://www.bloomsburyonlineresources.com/the-accent-handbook).*

R Variable:
Appearance of the R is less predictable, though an accent may follow a certain R pattern.
Pocket Coach: Pattern or random?
For instance, in this recording:
Sa**R**ah and **R**o**R**y c**R**uised their ba**R**ge
Listen to recording 8 *(https://www.bloomsburyonlineresources.com/the-accent-handbook).*

Remember! These recordings are of individual speakers. They don't represent an entire accent.

There are two R behaviours to listen out for:

Linking R:
R pronounced to help link between words.
Sarah and Rory cruised their barge **undeR a** narrow red bridge.
This allows the speaker to make a link when a word ends with an R in the spelling ('under') and the next word begins with a vowel sound ('a'). This can happen in rhotic, non-rhotic and R variable accents.
Listen to recording 9 *(https://www.bloomsburyonlineresources.com/the-accent-handbook).*

Inserted R:
R added between vowel sounds where it isn't written.
Sa**rah Rand** Rory cruised their barge under a narrow red bridge.

This can happen between words and also within words; for example, drawing can be pronounced draw**R**ing. Many rhotic accents would never do this, but some might, and it can happen in non-rhotic and R variable accents too.

Exercise: **Where the R?**

To help explore the accent's **R Type**
You need: an accent recording
See if you can make a type of R sound by putting these articulators together:

- top and bottom lip
- bottom lip and top front teeth
- tongue tip or blade and gum ridge
- tongue tip or blade and behind the gum ridge
- tongue tip and hard palate
- uvula and back of the tongue body

Play the accent recording, listening out for R sounds. When you hear one, pause the recording and imitate what you hear. What are you bringing together in the mouth to copy the sound? Are you making it sound the same? If it doesn't sound the same, what if you bring different articulators together?

Continue listening to the recording, pausing to copy Rs when you hear them, noticing where they're being made. Note down any discoveries.

If you notice more than one R Type, repeat the exercise to explore where this other R sound is made. Head to **R Tally** to see if you can find a pattern for when each R Type appears.

Exercise: **How the R?**

To help explore the accent's **R Type**
You need: an accent recording
Find space to move and listen to the recording, focusing on the R sounds. Listen carefully to them and mimic them as best you can. Does it sound like one articulator taps the other, or do they move towards each other but not touch? Do they trill?

Create a gesture that imitates the action. This action can be whatever you like, as long as it helps you connect to the type of obstruction. Listen to an accent recording again. Every time you hear an R sound, repeat the gesture and make the sound.

If you notice more than one R Type, repeat the exercise to explore how this other R sound is made. Head to **R Tally** to see if you can find a pattern for when each R appears.

Exercise: **R Tally**

*To help explore the accent's **R Range** and when each **R Type** appears*
You need: an accent recording, something to write with and on
Listen to your recording. When you come across the first R, stop, rewind and listen to it again to really hear it. Copy the sound as best you can. Call this 'R Type 1'.

Write 'R Type 1' down and put your first tally mark next to it. Now play your recording and every time you hear that R Type, add a tally mark. Have you put a mark for every R that is said? If yes, the accent has only one R Type and you know this R can be used for every R that is pronounced in the accent.

If there are more Rs to discover, listen again and when you hear a different type, write down 'R Type 2' and copy the sound as best you can. Every time you hear R Type 2, add a tally mark. If you hear a third, repeat the exercise with 'R Type 3' and so on.

If you've discovered more than one R Type, the next step is to find out when your speaker is making each one. There may not be a strict rule, but spelling could be a factor. Listen to your recording and this time, whenever you hear an R Type 1, write the word down.

Look at your list of words. Is there any correlation between the type of R and its position in the word? Does the R start the word, for example, or does it follow a consonant? Go through the same process for R Type 2 and so on. You may find little correlation between R Type and position, but if there is a pattern, that can be useful when applying the accent to text.

Retroflex Approximant:
Tip of the tongue curls back towards the hard palate but doesn't touch.
Pocket Coach: Retro = tongue goes back (in time)!
Listen to recording 14 *(https://www.bloomsburyonlineresources.com/the-accent-handbook)*.

Bunched Molar Approximant:
Back of the tongue raises as the whole tongue 'bunches' back. The sides of the tongue press against the molars.
Pocket Coach: think 'pirate'!
Listen to recording 15 *(https://www.bloomsburyonlineresources.com/the-accent-handbook)*.

Taps or Flaps:
Labiodental Tap:
Bottom lip moves to top front teeth, taps them and returns.
Pocket Coach: think very light 'V'.
Listen to recording 16 *(https://www.bloomsburyonlineresources.com/the-accent-handbook)*.

Alveolar Tap:
Tip or blade of the tongue moves to gum ridge, makes one tap and returns.
Pocket Coach: think very light 'd'.
Listen to recording 17 *(https://www.bloomsburyonlineresources.com/the-accent-handbook)*.

Retroflex Flap:
Tip of the tongue starts curled back. It moves forward and taps the hard palate.
Listen to recording 18 *(https://www.bloomsburyonlineresources.com/the-accent-handbook)*.

Trills:
Alveolar Trill:
Tip or blade of the tongue meets the gum ridge, finds the perfect amount of tension so that as the air blows through, the tip flutters multiple times.
Listen to recording 19 *(https://www.bloomsburyonlineresources.com/the-accent-handbook)*.

Uvular Trill:
Back of the tongue body makes contact with the uvula, finds the perfect amount of tension so that as the air blows through, the uvula flutters multiple times.
Pocket Coach: Think 'gargling R'.
Listen to recording 20 *(https://www.bloomsburyonlineresources.com/the-accent-handbook)*.

Fricatives:
Uvular Fricative:
Back of the tongue body moves very close to the uvula and air passes between them, creating a hissing sound.
Listen to recording 21 *(https://www.bloomsburyonlineresources.com/the-accent-handbook)*.

This isn't an exhaustive list of possibilities. These are examples of some of the more common R pronunciations in accents of English.

If the accent you're learning doesn't seem to make any of these, explore what is happening using the exercises in **Discovering R**.

Doing R

These exercises are to help you practise the accent's R sound/s:

Exercise: **R Buncher**

To help make a bunched molar R
You need: some text
This is the R Type you may hear in some American accents. It's called a 'Bunched Molar R' because the tongue quite literally bunches up and the sides touch the molar teeth. If you're struggling to make it, use this exercise to try different ways of approaching the task.

Make a long GRR sound as if you're an angry dog or bear. As you make the GRR, notice whether the sides of the tongue are touching your molar teeth. It might help to think of your tongue flattening and spreading wide. If you're not sure whether you're doing it, you can check by sliding your index finger in at the side of the mouth to feel whether the side of the tongue is touching the molars.

Sometimes thinking of an image can help. Imagine a pancake spreading out in a pan, for instance, or a magic carpet with the tassels stretching out to the sides. To bunch back, you could use the idea of waves crashing on a shoreline. The wave draws up and back before it crashes down. If these images don't work for you, feel free to explore your own to help create the up, back and braced movement.

Alternatively, making a movement or gesture along with the sound could help. Put your hand out in front of you, palm facing down. This is the tongue released, doing nothing. Now arch the hand up and back as you try a bunched molar R. You could do this move with your whole arm if it's more helpful.

Add the sound into your text. Start by working with words in isolation and work slowly. Use **Practice Makes Perrrrfect** to help get used to saying this R Type in different positions within words. You can also use **R Personality** to help connect to the sound even more.

Exercise: **R Tapper**

To help make an alveolar tap R
You need: some text
To make an alveolar tap, it can help to think of the R as a little light 'd' sound. Practise putting a little 'd' between two vowel sounds, like 'uh**d**uh'. Say this a few times, keeping the 'd' light and quick. Circle any words in your text where the accent might make an alveolar tap. They can often happen after consonant sounds or between vowels, as in these words:

> three, ap**r**on, ag**r**ee, st**r**aw, emb**r**ace, f**r**iend, d**r**y, sec**r**ets
> ve**r**y, mo**r**al, ma**rr**ied, cu**rr**y, si**r**en, ciga**r**ette, bea**r**ing, sto**r**age

Rewrite these words with a 'd', for instance: 'very' looks like 'vedy'. Practise saying the words with a very light 'd'. Make it the lightest you possibly can.

Add this sound into your text. Start by working with words in isolation and work slowly. Use **Practice Makes Perrrrfect** to help get used to saying this R Type in different situations. You can also use **R Personality** to help connect to the sound even more.

Exercise: **Triller Thriller**

To help make an alveolar trill R
You need: some text
It's a myth that being able to trill or 'roll' your R sound is genetic. The trick is to find a balance between tension in your tongue and strength in the airflow. Too little tension and the airflow has no resistance, too much tension and the tongue won't move when air is flowing, too much strength in the airflow and you will encourage extra tongue tension!

Release an out-breath to help expel excess tension. Practise putting a little 'd' between two vowel sounds, like 'uh**d**uh'. Say this a few times, keeping the 'd' light and quick. Keep the flow of air going and see if you can let the 'd' flutter in the airstream. If it doesn't, make micromovements with the tongue tip or blade. Bring it a little closer to the gum ridge, then a little further away. Find the sweet spot.

Think of the trill as 'thrilling'. Pretend you're using it to flirt or be cheeky, think of it as a fun, 'fluttery' sound. This is the sound Homer Simpson makes when he tries to seduce Marge! If you work too hard on it, you could add unneeded tension so try your best to maintain ease.

If you find yourself getting frustrated or tense, it can help to give it a rest! Let the tongue relax as you sigh out. Then try the trill again.

If this is the R Type in the accent, add it into your text. Start by working with words in isolation and work slowly. Use **Practice Makes Perrrrfect** to help get used to saying this R Type in different positions within words. You can also use **R Personality** to help connect to the sound even more.

Exercise: **R Gargler**

To help make a uvular trill R
You need: some text
This can help if the accent makes the R with a uvular trill and you're finding it tricky. Making a trill with the uvula and back of the tongue body can take some practice if you don't have this sound in your own accent. To make it more familiar, try gargling. This is the same action as the trill. Take a small sip of water, tip your head back and with an open mouth try a gentle gargle.

Now swallow the water and imitate the gargle, this time with air alone. If you find this difficult, gargle with water again to remind yourself of the action.

Once you have the action, add some sound. Practise this in isolation and then add it into words. The key is for it to sound effortless, so work to make it with ease. Add the sound into your text. Use **Practice Makes Perrrrfect** to help get used to saying this R Type in different positions within words. You can also use **R Personality** to help connect to the sound even more.

Exercise: **Leaving Lips Out**

To help stop the lips getting involved in making the R
You need: a mirror
This can be helpful if you make R sounds using your bottom lip, but the new accent uses only the tongue. Sit in front of the mirror with your jaw released and lips slightly parted. Put your finger gently on the bottom lip.

With your finger barring the lip, make a vowel sound of your choosing. Now add the movement of the tongue needed to make the R you're after. Go back and forth between vowel and R sound, focusing on the movement of the tongue.

Check your bottom lip. Can you feel it moving under your finger? Can you see it moving in the mirror? If it's trying to get involved, don't worry. Shake out and try again. Over time, you will get used to your tongue doing more of the work than your lips.

Once you're able to make the sound without lip movement under the finger, release it and try the R without any restraints. Watch in the mirror to make sure it doesn't get involved in producing the R. Add this sound into words in isolation and then into your script. Use **Practice Makes Perrrrfect** to help get used to saying this

R Type in positions within words. You can also use **R Personality** to help connect to the sound even more.

Rhotic accents

These exercises are to help practise Rs in rhotic accents.

Exercise: **The R Motorbike: Revving Rhotic**

To practise making every R in a rhotic accent
Inspired by the work of Annie Morrison
You need: some text

Sarah and **R**ory cruised thei**r** barge unde**r** a narrow, **r**ed bridge.

Remind yourself of the accent's R Type and practise it a few times. If the accent contains more than one R Type, decide which R you're going to use where in the phrase. **R Tally** may help with this.

Imagine you're on a motorbike. Hold the handlebars as you read the phrase through. Every time you get to an R in the spelling, 'rev' the throttle. If the sound can be lengthened, lengthen it. If it can't, make the action of revving at exactly the point you make the R to mark it with accuracy.

Practise making each R with energy, then reduce the amount of 'revving' so that you're still making them, but to a lesser extent to allow the phrase to flow. Take a line of your text and repeat the exercise by 'revving' every R that is written.

Exercise: **R Takeover**

To help increase strength and presence of the R in rhotic accents
You need: some text or your script
Let's say you need to make the R more often or more strongly for the accent, to give it more 'presence'. It could be that you find yourself losing the R sound at certain times or in particular words.

Remind yourself of the accent's R Type and practise it a few times. If the accent makes more than one type of R, pick one to start with and then repeat the exercise with another type.

Pick some lines or words where you feel the R drops out or could be stronger. Imagine the R is 'stitched on' or attached to the end of the vowel before it. Say the vowel with the R.

Now imagine that the R is taking over the 'territory' of the vowel, so when you say the word, the vowel has less space. Try it using these words:

mirror, party

Forget the vowels and let the Rs takeover completely! Move straight from the sound before the vowel to the R. Try this with other lines in your script and see if it helps give the R more strength and presence.

Exercise: **R Tongue Tanglers**

To practise Rs before other consonants
You need: something to write with and on, a highlighter
If your own accent is non-rhotic or R variable and the accent you're learning is rhotic, there may be certain words or phrases that you find difficult to say. Hitting Rs before consonants can be particularly tricky for some.

Remind yourself of the accent's R Type and practise it a few times. If the accent contains more than one R Type, decide which R you're going to use where in the following phrases. **R Tally** may help you with this.

Highlight every R written in the following sentences. Say each phrase slowly and be sure to make every R that is written:

That girl is the fourth person to look in the mirror.
I'll take your order shortly.
This generator really is the worst.
This excursion will require boardshorts.
Are you sure that's the girl we were talking about?
There are forty pages left in your journal.
The murderer's girlfriend was just around the corner.
It was a bittersweet departure.
My car's a convertible.

On a scale of 1 to 10, say the sentences as slowly as you possibly can at a level 1. Then gradually speed up to 2, 3, 4 and all the way up to 10 so that you're saying them as quickly as you can. If you miss out an R, take it down the speed scale.

Pick a sentence at random and imagine this is your one and only line in a film. Set the scene and deliver it as best you can in the accent.

Exercise: **Easeful R**

To help make Rs without excess effort
You need: some text
This exercise can help if you've learnt the Rs of the accent but you're making them sound too prominent or effortful.

Remind yourself of the accent's R Type/s and practise them a few times. Do this moving around your space to help release tension. Imagine you're using the sound to joke with someone.

Take a practice sentence or a few lines of text containing Rs. Circle any words where the R feels too effortful or strong. Speak the text in slow motion, as if you're walking on the moon or underwater. Keep it smooth and light.

For Rs before consonants (porch, work, cards etc.): imagine the R is 'stitched on' to the end of the vowel, as if they're one sound. Let the R take over the vowel, making the vowel feel shorter or smaller. By working less on making two separate sounds, you may find the R feels easier.

For Rs at the ends of words (over**r**, he**r**e, the**r**e etc.): say the word and release the R into a tiny little vowel sound (like an 'uh'). It might sound something like this: their(uh). Doing this may help clip or 'lift' the R and make it less effortful.

Exercise: **Painting Dropouts**

To help make Rs when the word or syllable isn't stressed in a rhotic accent
When the R is in a word or syllable that isn't stressed, you may find you accidentally drop it, especially when you're in full flow and heading for the next stress.

Look at the Rs in the following sentences. For this exercise, stress the <u>underlined</u> words. The Rs in **bold** are in unstressed words or syllables:

> I like you**r** <u>haircut</u>.
> She was born in <u>December</u>.
> Can I take you**r** <u>order</u>?
> Whe**re** are you**r** <u>friends</u>?
> You**r** <u>friends</u> are ove**r** <u>there</u>.
> Have eithe**r** the <u>chicken</u> o**r** <u>fish.</u>
> Is the game on <u>Saturday</u> o**r** <u>Sunday</u>?

Say the phrases through in your own accent first, making sure you stress the underlined words.

Imagine you're painting a canvas, paintbrush in hand. Say the sentences in the accent as best you can, and every time you get to the R, put a tiny dab of paint on the canvas. Make sure the dab really is a dab, not a giant splodge. Do this again at a faster pace. Now add some stakes or an intention to each sentence so you're acting rather than trying to make all the Rs!

Non-rhotic and R variable accents

These exercises are to help practise Rs in non-rhotic and R variable accents.

Exercise: **To R or Not to R?**

To help work out when to make an R in an R variable accent
You need: an accent recording
If you've discovered that the accent you're learning is R Variable, it might seem as though the Rs are being made randomly. This may be the case, but it can be useful to find out if there are patterns.

Listen to the accent recording for at least a minute and write down any words in which you hear the R sound being made. Highlight all the R sounds. Group them into the following:

> R at the start of words, e.g. raw, running, railings
> R at the end of words, e.g. or, winter, appear, here
> R before a consonant, e.g. shipyard, first, person

R after a consonant, e.g. crisp, through, strong
R between two vowel sounds, e.g. story, around, arrived

Have you got more words in one or two of these groups? Are there any groups which don't have any words in? Can you find a pattern for when to say them? If so, it can be useful to copy the patterns you find when applying the accent to text.

Exercise: **The R Motorbike: Revving Non-Rhotic and R Variable**

To practise only making Rs in certain positions
Inspired by the work of Annie Morrison
You need: some text
Remind yourself of the accent's R Type and practise it a few times. If the accent contains more than one R Type, decide which R you're going to use where in the phrase. **R Tally** may help you with this.

Sarah and **R**ory c**r**uised their barge under a na**rr**ow, **r**ed bridge.

For non-rhotic accents: Imagine you're on a motorbike. Hold the handlebars as you read the phrase. 'Rev' the throttle every time you come to an R that is followed by a vowel sound (Rs are in bold). If the sound can be lengthened, lengthen it. If it can't, make the action of revving at exactly the point you make the R.

Practise making each R in bold, then reduce the amount of 'revving' so that you're still making them, but to a lesser extent to allow the phrase to flow. Check that you aren't putting an R in 'their', 'barge' and 'under' (unless you are adding in a linking R here).

Repeat the exercise with a line of text. Make sure to only 'rev' Rs that are followed by a vowel sound.

For R variable accents: There may be less of a pattern for when the Rs are said. Try **To R or Not to R?** to help find a possible pattern and then mark the Rs in the phrase that you're going to make.

Practise making each of these Rs, then reduce the amount of 'revving' so that you're still making them, but to a lesser extent to allow the phrase to flow. Repeat the exercise with a line of your text.

Exercise: **Drop It Like It's Hot**

To help avoid saying certain Rs in non-rhotic or R variable accents
Before you start speaking, make sure you know where you need to drop the Rs. You could cross them out in your script or rewrite the word, so it doesn't have the R in the spelling anymore.

Imagine you have a ball of wastepaper in your hand which you're holding lightly. Speak your lines slowly. When you come to a word which needs a dropped R, hold out the imaginary ball of paper and drop it in the recycling. Or, if you prefer, get yourself a ball of paper and a bin and do the exercise literally.

Exercise: **Linking R Starts the Word**

To help add linking Rs in non-rhotic or R variable accents
If you're a rhotic speaker (you pronounce all your Rs) and you're learning a non-rhotic accent, it can be tempting to leave out linking Rs to avoid slipping back into your accent. However, if the new accent has them you will need them too, and this level of detail will make your performance more credible. Use the examples below:

fear is   sure about   near it   fair and

Linking Rs bridge the gap between two words. An easy way to link is to think of the R as starting the second word. You can even write it at the start:

Fear **Ris**   sure **Rabout**   near **Rit**   fair **Rand**

Say the second words on their own, then add the first words in. Search for linking Rs in your script and try the same technique.

Exercise: **R Hybrid Words**

To help embed linking Rs or inserted Rs in your script
Find some places for potential linking or inserted Rs in your script. Here are some examples:

Linking: fea**r** is   sure about
Inserted: raw **r**and crisp   area **r**around

Slowly say the two words linked by the R, feeling yourself making the R sound as you do so. Speed up a little so the two words flow together. It may start to sound like one word instead of two words. Does the new hybrid word give you an image? Does it sound like something else? Use this to make the hybrid word memorable.

Place it back in the line or phrase and speak it aloud. Write the hybrid word above the line or draw a symbol or doodle to help you remember it.

Exercise: **Practice Makes Perrrrfect**

To practise making the Rs you've noticed
Take the Rs you've noticed and practise making them in a variety of situations. If you've found more than one R Type, work out which is used where and practise them:

R on its own	e.g.	R
R – vowel	e.g.	Ra
Vowel – R	e.g.	eR
Vowel-R-vowel	e.g.	iRu
In a word	e.g.	Rory
In a phrase	e.g.	Sarah and Rory cruised their barge under a narrow, red bridge

If you're finding it difficult, make the sound in slow motion before gradually speeding up.

L

The L sound can be seen in words as follows:

Although Billy loved living in central Berlin, he literally longed for English trifle.

The L can be key if the new accent:

- pronounces the Ls differently from you = **L Type**
- has a different range of L Types to you = **L Range**

Discovering L

These exercises are to help work out how the accent pronounces Ls. If you already know what the accent does with Ls, head to the 'Doing L' section for practice.

Exercise: **Feel Your L**

*To help explore your own **L Type** and **L Range***
If you're not sure how and where you make your L sounds, slowly say these words:

letter

hello

well

Notice the movements and resistance to the airflow as you form the Ls. Make a hand movement, describe or draw a shape to remind you of what you felt. There is no need to go into detail here. You're simply becoming more aware of your **L Type**.

Say the words again slowly, focusing on the feel of the L sound. Does it feel the same every time you say it? Or are you making it slightly differently depending on where it is in a word? Say the words a few times and try to pronounce them as you usually would. You're becoming more aware of your **L Range**.

Exercise: **Where the L?**

*To help explore the accent's **L Type***
You need: an accent recording
See if you can make a type of L sound by putting these articulators together:

- top and bottom lip
- tongue tip or blade and gum ridge
- tongue tip or blade and behind the gum ridge
- tongue tip and hard palate
- front of the tongue body and hard palate

Play the accent recording, listening out for the L sounds. When you hear one, pause the recording and imitate what you hear. What are you bringing together in the mouth to copy the sound? Does it sound the same as the sound you heard? If it doesn't sound the same, what if you bring different articulators together?

Continue listening to the recording, pausing to copy Ls when you hear them, noticing where they're being made. Note down any discoveries.

If you notice more than one L Type, repeat the exercise to find out where this other type is made. Head to **Where in the Word for L?** to see if you can find a pattern for when each L Type appears.

Exercise: **How the L?**

*To help explore the accent's **L Type***
You need: an accent recording
Find space to move and listen to the recording, focusing on the L sounds. Listen carefully and try to mimic the action of the Ls in your mouth as best you can. Does it sound and feel like one articulator making firm contact with another, or do they move towards each other but not touch?

Create a gesture that imitates the action. This action can be whatever you like, as long as it helps you connect to the type of obstruction. Listen to the accent recording again. Every time you hear an L sound, repeat the gesture and make the sound.

Are all the L sounds made in the same way? If you hear more than one L Type, create a different gesture to imitate the different action. Head to **Where in the Word for L?** to see if you can find a pattern for when each L Type appears.

Exercise: **Where in the Word for L?**

*To help explore the accent's **L Range***
You need: an accent recording, something to write with and on
Play the accent recording, listening out for the L sounds. Do you hear different types of Ls being made? If you find it difficult to tell, it can help to listen a few times. If you do hear more than one L Type, there may be a pattern regarding the type and where the L is in the word.

Listen again. Write down words from the recording which have Ls in them. Find words with Ls in different places:

- start of a word   (loved, living)
- between two vowel sounds   (hello, literally)
- before a consonant sound   (although)
- after a consonant sound   (English)
- end of a word   (central, trifle)

With the words you've written in front of you, listen again. When you hear them in the recording, pause and imitate what you hear.

How do the Ls feel and sound? Do the Ls at the start of a word sound different from the ones at the end of a word? Notice and jot down any patterns. Leave your notes aside for a final listen and simply echo the L words when you hear them.

Doing L

These exercises are to help you practise the accent's L sound/s:

Exercise: **Find the Light**

To help make a light L sound
You need: some text
Begin by yawning to stretch and release the tongue. Let your jaw open slightly. Imagine the tip of your tongue is a delicate butterfly wing. Bring it to the alveolar

ridge and allow it to flutter against it (by making very light taps). As you do this light flutter with the tip or blade, keep the rest of the tongue released.

Make an 'AH' sound and repeat the gentle fluttering action to find this light L sound, keeping the middle of the tongue body released as you do so.

Change the vowel sound to an 'EE' and repeat the exercise. Then try it on an 'OO'. Certain vowels may make the light L more difficult to pronounce. If you find the quality of the L changes at any point, go back to the silent, gentle fluttering action you began with.

If this is the L Type in the accent, add it into your text. Start by working with words in isolation and work slowly. Use **Practice Builllllds Perfection** to help get used to saying this L Type in different positions within words. If the accent only makes light Ls in certain positions, use **Where in the Word for L?** to find out when to add this sound in.

Exercise: **The Dark Side**

To help make a dark L sound
You need: some text

Bring the middle of the tongue body up to the soft palate as if you're about to make a 'K' sound. Keep the middle of the tongue there. Put the tip or blade of your tongue on the gum ridge. Breathe in through your mouth. To do so, the middle of the tongue body will need to release from the soft palate. Allow this to happen, but keep it raised.

With the tongue in this position, make an 'AH' sound and then release the tongue tip down behind the bottom teeth. It may sound and feel a little like you're 'squeezing the sound', or that there is less space in the back of your mouth. Repeat this several times to find a dark L sound, keeping the middle of the tongue body raised as you do so.

If this is the L Type in the accent, add it into your text. Start by working with words in isolation and work slowly. Use **Practice Builllllds Perfection** to help get used to saying this L Type in different positions within words. If the accent only makes dark Ls in certain positions, use **Where in the Word for L?** to find out when to add this sound in.

Exercise: **The L Didgeridoo**

To help feel and move between light Ls and dark Ls
You need: some text

Place the tip or blade of your tongue on your gum ridge and say an 'AH' through the shape. Keep the middle and back of the tongue body released.

With the tip or blade of the tongue in the same place, bring the middle of the tongue body up towards the soft palate, as if 'closing the door'. Maintain the 'AH' as you do this.

Move back and forth between raising the middle of the tongue body and then lowering it while keeping the tip or blade on the gum ridge. It might help to think of the sound a didgeridoo makes. Can you find this quality?

With the middle of the tongue body raised, release the tongue tip to make a dark L. Add this sound into your text. 'Play' the L didgeridoo again, this time lowering the middle of the tongue. Release the tongue tip to make a light L and add it into your text. Can you hear and feel the differences any more clearly now?

Exercise: **Lippy Ls**

To help produce a lippy L sound
You need: some text
A lippy L is made with both lips and without the tongue at all. Make an AH sound and then round the lips so that they're creating the smallest circle, but not quite touching. You may recognize this as a type of 'W' sound. Say the word 'wow' a few times, noticing how the lips come together and spring apart.

Accents with lippy Ls tend to make them at the ends of words and before consonant sounds. For example, in the words 'ball', 'always' and 'falter'. Say the word 'ball', using the lippy L. It might feel as though you are saying 'baw'.

If this is an L Type in the accent, add it into your text. Go to **Where in the Word for L?** if you're unsure of where it features.

Exercise: **Practice Builllllds Perfection**

To help practise the Ls of the accent
Take the Ls you've noticed and practise making them in a variety of situations:

L on its own	e.g.	L
L – vowel	e.g.	La
Vowel – L	e.g.	eL
Vowel-L-vowel	e.g.	iLu
In a word	e.g.	aLong
In a phrase	e.g.	Although Billy loved living in central Berlin, he literally longed for English trifle

If you've found more than one L Type in the accent, use **Where in the Word for L?** to find out where each L Type is made and then use the relevant L for each position above.

If a particular position proves difficult, work slowly and gradually speed up until you're able to make the sound with ease.

TH

The TH can be seen in the words of the following sentence:

Think about **th**is: does your bro**th**er E**th**an brea**the th**rough
his nose or his mou**th**?

Although the TH is made up of two letters, when 'T' and 'H' are next to each other in spoken English, they're treated as one sound.

The TH can be key if the new accent:

- makes the THs differently to you = **TH Type**
- has a different range of TH Types to you = **TH Range**

Discovering TH

These exercises are to help work out how the accent pronounces THs. If you already know what the accent does with TH, head to the 'Doing TH' section for practice.

Exercise: **Feel Your TH**

*To help gain awareness of your own **TH Type** and **TH Range***
If you're not sure where and how you make your TH, slowly say these words:

thought
though
sou**th**
sou**th**ern

Notice the movements and resistance to the airflow as you form the TH sounds. Make a hand movement, describe or draw a shape to remind you of what you felt. There is no need to go into detail here. You're simply becoming more aware of your **TH Type**.

Say the words again slowly, focusing on the feel of the TH sound in each word. Does the sound feel the same every time? Or are you making it slightly differently depending on the word? Say the words again in this order:

thought
sou**th**
though
sou**th**ern

Did you say the first two words with a different TH to the second two? How many different types of TH did you make? Here, you're becoming more aware of your **TH Range**.

Exercise: **Where the TH?**

*To help explore the accent's **TH Type***
You need: an accent recording
See if you can make a type of TH sound by putting these articulators together:

- bottom lip and top front teeth
- tongue tip or blade and front teeth
- tongue tip or blade and gum ridge
- tongue tip or blade and behind the gum ridge
- tongue tip and hard palate

Play an accent recording, listening out for TH sounds. When you hear one, pause the recording and imitate what you hear. What are you bringing together in the mouth to copy the sound? Does it sound the same as the sound you heard? If it doesn't sound the same, what if you bring different articulators together?

Carry on listening to the recording, pausing to copy THs when you hear them, noticing where they're being made. Note any discoveries.

If you notice more than one type, repeat the exercise to find out where in the mouth the other TH Types are being made. Head to **Where in the Word for TH?** to see if you can find a pattern for when each TH Type appears.

Exercise: **How the TH?**

*To help explore the accent's **TH Type***
You need: an accent recording
Play the accent recording and listen out for the TH sounds. When you hear a TH, do you hear air 'exploding' out like a plosive or 'leaking' out like a fricative? If you're unsure, listen again and ask yourself if the THs seem short and clipped, or long and airy.

Listen once more. When you hear a TH, echo what you hear as closely as you can and work out if it's a short 'explosive' sound or a longer stream of air. To check, place your hand in front of your mouth. If you feel a sudden puff of air, it's likely you're making a plosive TH. If the stream of air can be sustained, it's likely you're making a fricative TH.

If you hear more than one TH Type, repeat the exercise to notice how it's made in the mouth. Head to **Where in the Word for TH?** to see if you can find a pattern for when each TH Type appears.

Exercise: **Good Vibrations?**

To help notice whether the accent has voiced and voiceless versions of TH
You need: an accent recording
Play the accent recording and listen out for the TH sounds. Copy the sounds you hear as closely as you can. Put your fingers gently on the front of your neck and notice whether you feel a vibration under your fingers as you make the sounds. If there is a vibration, the sound is voiced. If there is no vibration, the sound is voiceless – it's being powered by breath alone. If you're unsure, slow down and lengthen the TH sound as you make it.

Does the accent contain both voiced and voiceless TH sounds or are the THs always voiced, or always voiceless? Note down any discoveries.

Exercise: **Where in the Word for TH?**

To help explore the accent's **TH Range**

You need: an accent recording, something to write with and on

Play an accent recording, listening out for the TH sounds. Do you hear different types of THs being made? If you're not sure, it can help to listen a few times. If you do hear more than one TH Type, it might depend on where the TH is in the word.

Listen again. Write down some words from the recording which have THs in different places:

• Start of a word	(**th**ank, **th**at)
• Between two vowel sounds	(wea**th**er, bro**th**er)
• Before a consonant sound	(**th**rough)
• After a consonant sound	(heal**th**)
• End of a word	(ba**th**, ba**the**)

With the words you've written in front of you, listen again. When you hear them in the recording, pause and imitate what you hear.

How do the THs feel and sound? Are the TH sounds at the start of the word the same as the THs between two vowel sounds? Notice and jot down any patterns.

Leave your notes aside for a final listen and simply echo the TH words when you hear them.

Exercise: **TH Soundalike Swaps**

To help notice the accent's **TH Type**

You need: an accent recording, some text

Sometimes the TH Type can sound or feel like another sound. Play the accent recording and listen out for the TH sounds in words. If the TH sounds different to yours, does it remind you of any other sounds you make? Here are some possibilities:

F, V, T, D, S, Z, SH

Perhaps it doesn't sound like any of those but is like another sound you make. If so, note it down. Say a couple of TH words with the sound you heard your speaker make:

thought
though
sou**th**
sou**th**ern

If it helps, you can rewrite the words using the spelling of the sound you heard, for example **th**ought could be '**f**ought', '**s**ought' or '**t**ought'

Get your text and rewrite any words to help with pronunciation, and then read the text aloud.

Speech Bubble

The written TH tends to be pronounced in most accents of English. It would be very rare for it to be dropped. It's common for an accent to have two versions of TH: **voiced** and **voiceless**. For example:

then (tends to be voiced)
thin (tends to be unvoiced)

Even when there's no difference in where and how the TH is made in an accent, there will often be a voiced and voiceless version of the TH Type. This can vary depending on the accent.

It's especially worth listening out for the TH sound if you're learning an accent where the first language isn't English. When second language speakers come to English, they handle the TH in various ways.

Common TH types:

Voiced and Voiceless Fricatives:

Labiodental Fricative:
Lower lip meets the top front teeth, and a flow of air streams through, creating a hissing sound.
Pocket Coach: A type of F and V sound.
Listen to recording 25 *(https://www.bloomsburyonlineresources.com/the-accent-handbook)*.

Dental Fricative:
Tongue tip or blade meets either the sharp underside of the front teeth or the back of the top front teeth and a flow of air streams through, creating a hissing sound.
Pocket Coach: 'toothy tongue poke'!
Listen to recording 26 *(https://www.bloomsburyonlineresources.com/the-accent-handbook)*.

Alveolar Fricative:
Tongue tip or blade meets the gum ridge, and a flow of air streams through, creating a hissing sound.
Pocket Coach: A type of S and Z sound.
Listen to recording 27 *(https://www.bloomsburyonlineresources.com/the-accent-handbook)*.

Voiced and Voiceless Plosives:

Dental Plosive:
Tongue tip or blade meets the back of the front teeth; air builds up behind and explodes through.
Listen to recording 28 *(https://www.bloomsburyonlineresources.com/the-accent-handbook)*.

Doing TH

These exercises are to help you practise the accent's TH sound/s:

Exercise: **Toothy Tongue Poke**

To help make a dental fricative TH
You need: some text
This TH Type doesn't appear in many languages and accents, and for that reason it can be difficult to produce with ease and consistency if it isn't your habitual sound. If you're having trouble, try this exercise.

　　Clean your upper front teeth with your tongue tip. Get used to the hard feel of the teeth against the tongue. Using the blade of your tongue, feel the sharp edge of the top front teeth. Run the blade from side to side, then back to the centre.

　　Now make an S sound and slowly move the tongue forward until you feel the tongue tip gently touching the back of the top front teeth. Your tongue may start to appear between your top and bottom teeth. This is the voiceless version of the sound. For the voiced version, start by making a 'Z' and repeat the action of moving the tongue forward.

　　Say the phrase with these TH sounds. It may help to think of a lizard, with the tongue darting forward as if it's catching flies at the entrance to the mouth!

*Does your bro**th**er E**th**an brea**th**e **th**rough his nose or his mou**th**?*

Start slowly, then gradually speed up. Speakers with a toothy tongue poke TH tend to bring their tongue either behind or between the teeth. Use whichever feels most comfortable for you. Use **Practice MakeTH Perfection** to help get used to saying this TH Type in different positions within words. Add it into your text.

Exercise: **Punch Your TH**

To help make a plosive TH

Let's say the accent makes a TH Type which is shorter and more explosive than yours. Work out the TH Type for the accent (using **Where the TH?** and **What the TH?** to help). Bring the articulators together to make the accent's TH and imagine you've glued them there. Go to make the sound but keep your articulators glued together. Allow the air to burst through to create an explosion. Repeat this a few times to practise.

Continue to make this sound but make a punching gesture at the same time. Make the sound match the strong, quick action. Try making voiced and voiceless versions of this TH Type. Take your text and add this sound in where appropriate. Use **Practice MakeTH Perfection** to help get used to saying this TH Type in different words.

Exercise: **Air Your TH Out**

To help make fricative THs

Let's say the accent makes a TH Type which is longer and 'airier' than yours. Work out the TH Type for the accent and bring the relevant articulators together. Try **Punch Your TH** first to find a plosive action. Reduce the muscular effort so that the articulators 'rest' on one another. Send air through the articulators. Allow the air to bring the articulators slightly apart so that it hisses through. Think of popping a bike tyre and the air escaping out. Place your hand in front of your mouth so that you can feel the flow of air as it passes through. If you're making a voiceless version, add voice to find a voiced version too, or vice versa.

An alternative way is to think of the SH sound you might make to tell someone to be quiet. Make the sound and notice the quality. Try to recreate this sound but with the articulators required for the accent's TH Type. Can you find the same airy quality? Try a voiced and a voiceless version of this TH Type.

Use **Practice MakeTH Perfection** to help get used to saying this TH Type in different positions in words, then add it into your text.

Exercise: **Practice MakeTH Perfection**

To practise making the TH sounds you've noticed

Take the THs you've noticed and practise making them in a variety of situations:

TH on its own	e.g.	TH
TH – vowel	e.g.	THa
Vowel – TH	e.g.	eTH
Vowel-TH-vowel	e.g.	iTHu
In a word	e.g.	THree
In a phrase	e.g.	Think about this: Does your brother Ethan breathe through his nose or his mouth?

If you've noticed more than one TH Type in the accent, use **Where in the Word for TH?** to find out where each TH Type is made and then use the relevant TH for each position above. If you're finding it difficult, make the sound in slow motion before gradually speeding up. Try making voiced and voiceless versions of the TH Type.

T

The T sound can be seen in words as follows:

Twen**t**y-**t**wo li**tt**le bo**tt**les sa**t** ou**t** on the pa**t**io

The T can be key if the accent:

- makes T sounds differently from you = **T Type**
- makes a different range of T sounds to you = **T Range**

Discovering T

These exercises are to help work out how the accent pronounces Ts. If you already know what the accent does with Ts, head to the 'Doing T' section for practice.

Exercise: **Feel Your T**

*To help gain awareness of your **T Type** and **T Range***
If you're not sure how and where you make your T sounds, slowly say these words:

two
fi**tt**er
ba**t**

Notice the movements and resistance to the airflow as you form the T sounds. Make a hand movement, describe or draw a shape to remind you of what you felt. There is no need to go into detail here. You're simply becoming more aware of your **T Type**.

Say the words again slowly, focusing on the feel of the T sound. Does it feel the same every time you say it? Or are you making it slightly differently depending on where it is in a word? Here, you're becoming more aware of your **T Range**.

Exercise: **Spot Your Ts**

*To help notice your **T Type***
You need: a recording device
Some speakers of English will use only one T Type, while others use several T Types in their speech. Read the following in your own accent:

It's hot out today. Come out of the sun and get me some water. Cut up a tomato from the basket of vegetables on the table. Add it to the pot with some butter. I don't mind if it's too tangy. I've put the button back on your shirt. Wear that one to dinner tonight.

You might pronounce Ts differently when reading than you would usually. This is because T pronunciation has long been associated with so-called 'standard' or 'proper' ways of pronouncing written English, especially in the United Kingdom. Try to shake this off!

Record yourself saying the lines faster, and as if talking to an old friend. This may help you to pronounce the Ts as you would habitually. Listen back and notice how many different T Types you made. Note down any discoveries.

Exercise: **Where the T?**

*To help explore the accent's **T Type***
You need: an accent recording
See if you can make a type of T sound by putting these articulators together:

- tongue tip or blade and top front teeth
- tongue tip or blade and gum ridge
- tongue tip or blade and behind the gum ridge
- tongue tip and hard palate
- vocal folds

Play the accent recording, listening out for T sounds. When you hear one, pause the recording and imitate what you hear. What are you bringing together in the mouth to copy the sound? Does it sound the same as the sound you heard? If it doesn't, what if you bring different articulators together?

Carry on listening to the recording, pausing to copy Ts when you hear them and noticing where they're being made. Note any discoveries.

If you notice more than one type being made, repeat the exercise to find out where in the mouth the other T Types are being made. Head to **Where in the Word for T?** to see if you can find a pattern for when each T Type appears.

Exercise: **How the T?**

*To help explore the accent's **T Type***
Play an accent recording and listen for the T sounds. When the Ts are made, do you hear air 'exploding' out or 'leaking' out? If you're unsure, listen again and ask yourself if the Ts seem short and sudden, or longer and airier.

Listen again. When you notice a T, echo what you hear and work out if it's a short 'explosive' sound or a longer stream of air by placing your hand in front of your mouth. If you feel a sudden puff of air, it's likely you're making a plosive sound. If the stream of air can be sustained, it's likely you're making a fricative sound.

Are all the T sounds made in the same way? If you hear more than one T Type, head to **Where in the Word for T?** to see if you can find a pattern for when each T Type appears.

Exercise: **Where in the Word for T?**

*To help explore the accent's **T Range***
You need: an accent recording, something to write with and on
In some accents, T sounds can be made differently depending on where they are within a word. Play the accent recording, listening out for the T sound. Do you hear

different T Types being made? If you're not sure, listen again. Write down some words from the recording which have Ts in different positions in the word:

- Start of a word   (**t**en, **t**ree)
- Between two vowel sounds   (ho**tt**er, cu**tt**ing)
- Before a consonant sound   (fi**t**ful)
- After a consonant sound   (des**t**iny)
- End of a word   (abou**t**, respec**t**)

With the words you've written in front of you, listen again. When you hear them in the recording, pause and imitate what you hear.

How do the Ts feel and sound? Do the Ts at the start of a word sound different from the ones at the end of a word? Notice and jot down any patterns. Leave your notes aside for the final listen and simply echo the T words when you hear them.

Speech Bubble

Common T types:

Voiced and Voiceless Plosives:
Dental Plosive:
Tongue tip or blade meets the top front teeth; air builds up and explodes through.
Listen to recording 30 *(https://www.bloomsburyonlineresources.com/the-accent-handbook)*.

Alveolar Plosive:
Tongue tip or blade meets the gum ridge; air builds up and explodes through.
Listen to recording 31 *(https://www.bloomsburyonlineresources.com/the-accent-handbook)*.

Retroflex Plosive:
Tongue tip curls back to meet the hard palate; air builds up and explodes through.
Listen to recording 32 *(https://www.bloomsburyonlineresources.com/the-accent-handbook)*.

Glottal Plosive:
Vocal folds come together, air builds up under them and explodes through. (You may have heard this referred to as a 'glottal stop'.)
Pocket Coach: initial sounds in uh-oh.
Listen to recording 33 *(https://www.bloomsburyonlineresources.com/the-accent-handbook)*.

Glottal Reinforcement:
Vocal folds come together, air builds up under them and explodes through as a dental, alveolar or retroflex plosive is made either simultaneously or immediately after.

Doing T

These exercises are to help you make the accent's T sound/s:

Exercise: **Lessen the Leak**

To help make voiceless plosive Ts and to reduce aspiration ('airiness')
You need: a piece of paper, some text
This exercise can be useful if the accent makes plosive T sounds, or the T sounds are less aspirate than yours.

To find a plosive sound, imagine you have a blob of glue sticking together the two articulators used to make the sound. Go to produce a T sound but don't allow the glue to come unstuck. Allow them to come apart, creating only a very small puff of air.

Twenty-two li**tt**le bo**tt**les sa**t** ou**t** on the patio.

Say the phrase in the accent. Every time you get to a T sound, glue the articulators together and then release them with a very small puff of air.

Another way to make a plosive T is to think of it as a D. Change the phrase to:

Dwen**d**y **d**wo li**dd**le bo**ddl**es sa**d** ou**d** on the pa**d**io.

Say the phrase with these D sounds. Make the Ds in the same place in the mouth as you make the Ts for this accent. Then say it with Ts, not Ds, keeping some of the 'D quality'.

If you find there is still too much aspiration when you make the T, try saying the phrase with a piece of paper in front of your mouth. Your goal is to make the Ts but not to move the paper with air. Once you've made a plosive T with either less or no aspiration, add the sound to your text.

Exercise: **T Puff**

To help make aspirated ('airy') Ts
You need: some text, a piece of paper
This exercise can be useful if the accent makes T sounds with more aspiration than you.

Make a T and then make a small H. Make the sounds separately and then try to make them as close together as possible, so that they're almost happening simultaneously.

Place your hand in front of your mouth and say the phrase with this T + H. Every time you make the T sound, try your best to 'fire' the consonant into your hand by giving an extra puff of air after it. If you feel a strong puff of air, you've aspirated the T.

Twenty-two li**tt**le bo**tt**les sa**t** ou**t** on the patio.

Say the phrase in the accent, focusing on the T sounds. Every time you get to a T sound, add the little H sound immediately after it.

You can also try this exercise with a piece of paper in front of your mouth. Your goal is to move the piece of paper every time you make a T sound. Once you've moved the paper for every T, practise reducing the aspiration so it's still there, but the phrase can flow. If this is the T Type in the accent, practise adding it into your text.

Exercise: **T Cymbal**

To help make affricate Ts
You need: some text
This exercise can be useful if the accent makes T sounds with more affrication than you, but they're not quite fricatives.

Imagine you're sitting behind a drum kit. Take an imaginary drumstick and play the high hat by making a TS. Make a series of TS, TS, TS sounds.

Twenty-**t**wo li**tt**les sa**t** ou**t** on the patio.

Say the phrase, making a TS for every written T. If it helps, continue to 'play' the TS. If this is the T Type in the accent, practise adding it into your text. You can even rewrite the words with TS to help remind you.

Exercise: **Airing out the T**

To help make fricative Ts
You need: some text
This exercise can be useful if the accent makes fricative Ts and you don't.

Twenty-**t**wo li**tt**le bo**tt**les sa**t** ou**t** on the patio

Rewrite the phrase so that the Ts are replaced with S. Not TS like in **T Cymbal**, but S.

Swen**s**y **s**wo li**ss**le bo**ss**les sa**s** ou**s** on the pa**s**io.

Say the phrase as it is written. This may not sound exactly like the accent, but it's good practice for fricative Ts. Use **Where in the Word for T?** to find out which T sounds are fricatives in the accent, then add this sound to your text where appropriate.

Exercise: **Diddly D**

To help voice a T
You need: something to write with and on, some text
This can be helpful if the accent voices Ts in certain positions and you don't.
Take the words 'little', 'bottles' and 'patio' and rewrite the Ts as Ds.

li**dd**le, bo**dd**les, pa**d**io

Say the words above as they're written, making Ds not Ts.

Twenty-two li**dd**le bo**dd**les sa**d** ou**d** on the pa**d**io.

Say the phrase in the accent, replacing Ts with Ds in all the positions indicated. Use **Where in the Word for T?** to find out which T sounds are voiced in the accent and rewrite them as Ds in your text. Practise saying them out loud.

Exercise: **Silent Retreat Cough**

To help make a glottal plosive T
You need: some text
This can be helpful if the accent makes a T as a glottal stop in certain positions and you don't.
Start by imitating a cough. Notice how this feels. Do this several times, each time making the cough smaller. Make the smallest cough you can, as if you have to clear

your throat at a silent retreat. If you're bringing the vocal folds together so that air builds up under them and then blows them apart, you're making a glottal plosive.

Say the phrase 'uh-oh', making this small cough-like sound at the beginning of 'uh' and 'oh'. Take the words 'little', 'bottles' and 'patio' and make this sound where the T is written. Now add the little cough-like sound into the phrase:

Twenty-two little bottles sat out on the patio.

Use **Where in the Word for T?** to find out which T sounds are glottalled in the accent, then add this sound to your text where appropriate.

Exercise: **Glottal Hitch**

To help practise glottal reinforcement Ts
This can be helpful if the accent makes a glottal plosive together with another plosive. The glottal is 'reinforced' by the plosive that occurs either simultaneously or immediately after it.

Just as in **Silent Retreat Cough**, say the phrase 'uh-oh' feeling a small cough-like sound or 'hitch' between the words. This is a glottal plosive. Say the word 'pretty', using this sound for the TT. Then say the word 'too', making the T with the tip or blade of your tongue exploding off the gum ridge. This is an alveolar plosive.

We're going to put these two sounds together in the word 'pretty'. It can be useful to think of the word as two separate parts – 'pret' and 'ty'. For the first part, use the glottal plosive (silent retreat cough) for the T. For the second part, use the alveolar plosive for the T. You're 'reinforcing' the glottal sound with the other plosive sound.

Add these two sounds into the words 'twenty', 'bottle' and 'patio', then into the phrase:

Twenty-two little bottles sat out on the patio.

Use **Where in the Word for T?** to help explore which T sounds are glottal reinforcements in the accent, then add them to your text where appropriate.

Exercise: **Practice Makes Tottttttal Perfection**

To practise making the T sounds you've noticed
Take the Ts you've noticed and practise making them in a variety of situations.

T on its own	e.g.	T
T – vowel	e.g.	Ta
Vowel – T	e.g.	eT
Vowel-T-vowel	e.g.	iTu
In a word	e.g.	beTTer
In a phrase	e.g.	Twenty-two little bottles sat out on the patio

If you've noticed more than one T Type, use **Where in the Word for T?** to find out where each T Type is made and then use the relevant T for each position above. If you're finding it difficult, slow right down before gradually speeding up.

H

The H sound can be seen in the following words:

Hamish and **H**amoud **h**ated **h**aving **h**olidays in **H**ull.

The H can be key if the accent:

- makes the H more or less frequently than you = **H Number**
- makes the H differently to you = **H Type**

Discovering H

These exercises are to help work out how the accent pronounces Hs. If you already know what the accent does with Hs, head to the 'Doing H' section for practice.

Exercise: **Feel Your H**

*To help gain awareness of your own **H Type***
If you're not sure how and where you make your H sounds, say these words:

have
be**h**ind

Notice any movements and resistance you may make to the airflow as you form the H sounds. Make a hand movement, describe or draw a shape to remind yourself of what you felt. There is no need to go into detail here. You're simply becoming more aware of your **H Type**. Say the following a few times:

hand
and

Are you saying the words in exactly the same way, or are you making an H at the start of 'hand'? Here, you're becoming more aware of your **H Number**.

Exercise: **Spot Your Hs**

*To help notice your **H Number***
You need: a recording device
Some speakers of English say more H sounds than others; however, it's incredibly rare for a speaker to pronounce every single written H. Read the following in your own accent:

Who is **H**enry **H**olden? **H**e's the **h**eir. On my **h**onour. When's **h**e arriving? They said in an **h**our, but I don't know w**h**ether **h**e is, or **h**e's **h**ad an ex**h**aust problem. W**h**at kind of vehicle does **h**e **h**ave? Is **h**e **h**onest? **H**e's coming up the **h**ill now. **H**ave you finished? You must **h**ave.

You might find that you say more Hs when reading than we would usually. This is because H pronunciation has long been associated with so-called standard or 'proper' ways of pronouncing written English. Try to shake this off!

Record yourself saying the lines faster, and as if talking to an old friend. This may help you to pronounce the Hs as you would habitually. Listen back and circle the Hs you heard yourself make. If you just heard a vowel where the H was written, the H wasn't made. For example, did you say: 'You **must have**' or 'You **must've**'?

Is there a pattern regarding when you did and didn't say an H? Did you say them at the start of words, for instance, or did it depend on what words you were stressing in the sentence? Note down any discoveries.

Exercise: **H or Vowel?**

*To help explore the accent's **H Number***

Play the accent recording, listening out for words with a written H in them. To begin with, it can be helpful to listen for words that begin with an H (hello, horse, had etc.). Write these words down.

Listen again and focus on these words. Do you just hear a vowel sound, or do you hear some form of resistance to the airflow in the speaker's voice? If there is resistance, they're making some kind of H. Whenever you think you hear an H sound, raise your finger or hand in response to help mark it.

Listen more than once. When you hear an H in a word, allow yourself to gently echo that word, imitating the H as closely as you can.

Overall, do you feel as though they made an H sound more or less than you do? Did they say it where you wouldn't say it, or vice versa? If you noticed any particular patterns for Hs that are different from your own, write them down.

Exercise: **Where the H?**

*To help explore the accent's **H Type***
You need: an accent recording

See if you can make a type of H sound by putting these articulators together:

- Middle of the tongue body and soft palate
- Back of the tongue body and uvula
- Root of the tongue and pharynx
- Vocal folds

Play the accent recording, listening out for the H sounds. When you hear one, pause the recording and imitate what you hear. What are you bringing together in the mouth to copy the sound? Does it sound the same as the sound you heard? If it doesn't, what if you bring different articulators together?

Carry on listening to the recording, pausing to copy Hs when you hear them, noticing where they're being made. If you notice more than one H Type, repeat the exercise to find out where this new type is made.

Are there any patterns regarding when a particular H Type is made? Listen to your recording again and note down when you hear which type. Is it related to whether or not that word is stressed? Note down any observations.

Exercise: **How the H?**

*To help explore the accent's **H Type***
You need: an accent recording

Find space to move and listen to the recording, focusing on the H sounds. Listen carefully and try to mimic the action of the Hs in your mouth as best you can.

Create a gesture that imitates the action. This action can be whatever you like, as long as it helps you connect to the type of obstruction.

Listen to the accent recording again. Every time you hear an H sound, repeat the gesture and make the sound. Are all the H sounds made in the same way? If you hear more than one H Type, create a different gesture to imitate the different action.

Are there any patterns regarding when a particular H Type is made? Listen to your recording again and note down when you hear which type. Is it related to whether or not that word is stressed? Note down any observations.

Speech Bubble

Hs in accents of English are often voiceless fricatives of some kind.

Common H types:

Voiceless Fricatives:

Velar Fricative:
Middle of the tongue body comes very close to the soft palate and a flow of air streams through, creating a hissing sound.
Listen to recording 38 *(https://www.bloomsburyonlineresources.com/the-accent-handbook)*.

Uvular Fricative:
Back of the tongue body comes very close to the uvula and a flow of air streams through, creating a hissing sound.
Listen to recording 39 *(https://www.bloomsburyonlineresources.com/the-accent-handbook)*.

Pharyngeal Fricative:
Tongue root moves very close to the back wall of the pharynx (throat) and a flow of air streams through, creating a hissing sound.
Listen to recording 40 *(https://www.bloomsburyonlineresources.com/the-accent-handbook)*.

Glottal Fricative:
Vocal folds come very close to each other and a flow of air streams through, creating a huffing sound.

Listen to recording 41 *(https://www.bloomsburyonlineresources.com/the-accent-handbook)*.

Common H behaviours:

Silent H:
Not every written H in English is pronounced. Some words have a silent H at the beginning, before a vowel:

hour

heir

They're not often pronounced at the end of a word and they may not be made between vowels:

cheeta**h**

anni**h**ilate

Listen to recording 42 *(https://www.bloomsburyonlineresources.com/the-accent-handbook)*.

H Dropping:
Some accents of English pronounce **fewer** written Hs than others. It usually happens at the start of a word or syllable:

'ave you 'eard the news?

Listen to recording 43 *(https://www.bloomsburyonlineresources.com/the-accent-handbook)*.

H Insertion:
Some accents of English **add** H sounds where they aren't written:

He'll be comin' of **h**age this 'ay 'arvest.

(*Adam Bede* by George Eliot)

Listen to recording 44 *(https://www.bloomsburyonlineresources.com/the-accent-handbook)*.

This isn't an exhaustive list of possibilities. These are examples of some of the more common pronunciations in accents of English.

If the accent you're learning doesn't seem to make any of these, explore what is happening using the exercises in **Discovering H**.

Doing H

These exercises are to help you practise the accent's H sound/s:

Exercise: **H Dropping**

To help drop Hs
You need: some text

This can be useful if the accent drops the H sounds more than you. Take the sentence below:

Hamish and **H**amoud **h**ated **h**aving **h**olidays in **H**ull.

Say the sentence with no H sounds at all, simply say the vowels after them. Does this sound like the accent? If so, take your text and simply cross out all the H letters to remind yourself not to make any of them (this doesn't include TH and SH spelling as these are considered to be single speech sounds).

Some accents do not drop all H sounds. Listen back to your recording and notice when the speaker drops the H from a word. There may be a pattern which you can use as a guide. If the accent drops all Hs, it might help to do the following:

Insert an R sound:

the cheetah **R** 'ad half an hour to arrive

Make an **a/an** switch:

They're selling **a** house
becomes . . .
They're selling **an** 'ouse

Exercise: **H Adding**

To help add Hs

This exercise can be useful if the new accent pronounces more H sounds than you. Make the H sound for the accent. Check that you're bringing the relevant articulators together. Give this H sound a gesture. It can be something that reminds you of the sound or something abstract. Say the following words.

hello, holiday, hamster

As you say the words, say the Hs strongly and make the gesture with level 10 commitment. Then do the same with the phrase:

Hamish and **H**amoud **h**ated **h**aving **h**olidays in **H**ull.

Make the same gesture but only with your index finger. Make it very small and precise. Say the phrase again with this tiny gesture, and allow the Hs to be smaller, but still there. Add this H sound into your text.

Exercise: **Easy H**

To help make H sounds without excess effort
You need: a mirror, some text

Let's say the new accent pronounces H sounds more than you, but you find yourself adding them in 'heavily', with so much effort it's affecting the flow of speech. Try this exercise.

Stand or sit in front of a mirror or window so you can see your breath on the glass. If you don't have one, imagine you're in front of a window on a cold winter's day.

Release your shoulders and let your arms fall to your side. Have a big, wide yawn. Start a gentle laugh, either a haha, heehee or huhuh. You'll see your breath on the glass or mirror but keep the breath gentle and easy, so it doesn't steam up too strongly. Move onto some other vowels, keeping the gently bubbling laugh going.

If the accent has glottal fricative Hs, then you have found them with this laugh. If you've noticed a different H Type, bring the relevant articulators together and 'laugh' through them. Find the laugh gently.

Without losing the easeful sensation, slow down by lengthening the vowel sounds. Check in the mirror or glass to see if your breath has become stronger. If it has suddenly increased in strength and pressure, go back to the gentle laugh.

Move from long vowels to saying words starting with H. Then some words with H in the middle. Put them into a phrase. Keep your eye on the glass to keep your breath easy and gentle. Add these easy Hs into your text.

Exercise: **Airy H**

To help make H sounds with more air
You need: a piece of paper, some text
This exercise can be helpful if the accent you're learning adds a little more air to the Hs than you do.

Hamish and Hamoud hated having holidays in Hull.

Say the phrase once through in the accent, focusing on the H sounds. Check that you're bringing the relevant articulators together.

Hold the piece of paper in front of your mouth and make the H sound. Your goal is to move the paper with your H, so you need some breath here!

Say the phrase, aiming to move the paper for each of the H sounds. How do the Hs sound now? Have you managed to give them a little more air?

Put the paper to one side but keep the energy you found for the Hs and repeat the phrase with this 'airier' H. Read your text, adding this sound for the Hs where appropriate.

Exercise: **Smooth the Edges**

To help avoid glottal attack when H dropping
Let's say the accent you're learning drops Hs, but you've found that without the cushioning of an H sound, you're landing quite heavily on the vowels. This could

create a 'hard' sound known as 'glottal attack' which might not work for the accent. This exercise may help.

Start with a big sigh. Do several of these to release any excess tension. Sigh and then move into saying the following words, sighing before each one:

hello

horse

hotel

Make the sigh silent. Add this silent sigh to the beginning of the words. Have you managed to reduce the glottal attack? Do this a few times to get used to the action.

Highlight the words in your text where Hs need to be dropped. Sigh onto them, and then silent sigh onto them to help smooth the edges.

Exercise: **Practice Helps Not Hinders Perfection**

To practise making the H sounds you've noticed
Take the Hs you've noticed and practise making them in a variety of situations. If the accent doesn't make the Hs in all these situations, skip them!

H on its own	e.g.	H
H – vowel	e.g.	Ha
Vowel-H-vowel	e.g.	iHu
In a word	e.g.	beHave
In a phrase	e.g.	Hamish and Hamoud hated having holidays in Hull

If you're finding it difficult, make the sound in slow motion before gradually speeding up.

NG

The NG sound can be seen in the following words:

The ki**ng** was danci**ng** and si**ng**i**ng** all night lo**ng**.

Although the NG is seen as two spelling characters, 'N' and 'G', they are treated as one sound when written together.

The NG can be key if the accent:

- makes the NG differently to you = **NG Type**
- makes a different range of NG sounds to you = **NG Range**

Discovering NG

These exercises are to help work out how the accent pronounces NGs. If you already know what the accent does with NGs, head to the 'Doing NG' section for practice.

Exercise: **Feel Your NG**

*To help gain awareness of your own **NG Type***
If you're not sure how and where you make your NG sounds, slowly say these words:

si**ng**

si**ng**er

si**ng**i**ng**

Notice the movements and resistance to the airflow as you form the NG sounds. Make a hand movement, describe or draw a shape to remind you of what you felt. There is no need to go into detail here. You're just becoming slightly more aware of your NG Type.

Say the words again slowly, focusing on the feel of the NG sound. Does the sound feel the same every time? Or are you making it slightly differently depending on where it is in a word? Read the following aloud:

What've you been doi**ng**? I've been ba**ng**i**ng** on the swi**ng** door for so lo**ng**! I tried calli**ng** and ri**ng**i**ng** the bell. No, I'm not a**ng**ry, I'm runni**ng** to the store – do you need anythi**ng** picki**ng** up? Stri**ng** or chewi**ng** gum? Your kids are playi**ng** down alo**ng** the stream catchi**ng** fish. Ha**ng** on, are you seei**ng** this? The baby's grabbi**ng** my fi**ng**er. Amazi**ng**! Right, I'm goi**ng** out now.

We might say NGs differently when reading than we would when simply speaking.

Record yourself saying the following lines faster and as if talking to an old friend. Listen back to how you're making those NGs. Are you making them all in the same way or are there differences? Note any discoveries.

Exercise: **Where the NG?**

*To help explore the accent's **NG Type***
You need: an accent recording
See if you can make a type of NG sound by putting these pairs of articulators together:

- Tip or blade of the tongue and gum ridge
- Middle of the tongue body and soft palate
- Back of the tongue body and uvula

Play the accent recording, listening out for the NG sounds. When you hear one, pause the recording and imitate what you hear. What are you bringing together in the mouth to copy the sound? Does it sound the same as the sound you heard? If it doesn't, what if you bring different articulators together?

Carry on listening to the recording, pausing to copy NGs when you hear them, noticing where they're being made. If you notice more than one NG Type, repeat the exercise to find out where this new type is made. Note down any discoveries.

Exercise: **How the NG?**

*To help explore the accent's **NG Type***
You need: an accent recording
Find a space with room to move and listen to the recording, focusing on the NG sounds. Listen carefully and try to mimic the action of the NGs in your mouth as best you can. Does it feel like the articulators meet for the entirety of the sound, or do they release before the end, creating a puff of air?

Create a gesture that imitates the action. This action can be whatever you like, as long as it helps you to connect to the type of obstruction. Are all the NG sounds made in the same way? If you hear more than one NG Type, create a different gesture to imitate the different action.

Listen to the accent recording again. Every time you hear an NG sound, repeat the gesture and make the sound.

Exercise: **Where in the Word for NG?**

*To explore the accent's **NG Range***
You need: an accent recording, something to write with and on
NG sounds might be made differently depending on where they are within a word. Play the accent recording, listening out for the NG sound. Do you hear different types of NGs being made or does the speaker use the same sound every time? It can help to listen again if you're unsure.

Write down some words from the recording which have NGs in different positions in the word:

- Between two vowel sounds   (si**ng**er, Birmi**ng**ham)
- Before a consonant sound   (E**ng**land)
- End of a word   (walki**ng**, helpi**ng**)

With the words you've written in front of you, listen again. When you hear them in the recording, pause and imitate what you hear. How do the NGs feel and sound? Notice any patterns. Do the NGs between two vowel sounds sound different from the NGs at the end of the words?

By listening and copying in this way you can establish any patterns the accent has for making NGs. Leave your notes aside for the final listen and simply echo the NG words when you hear them.

Speech Bubble

Common NG types:

All NG sounds begin voiced, meaning the vocal folds come together and vibrate and all NG sounds are nasals, meaning the sound travels down the nose.

Nasals:
Alveolar Nasal:
Tip or blade of the tongue is on the gum ridge. The soft palate lowers so the air flows out through the nose.
Pocket Coach: Think 'N'.
Listen to recording 45 *(https://www.bloomsburyonlineresources.com/the-accent-handbook)*.

Velar Nasal:
Soft palate meets the middle of the tongue body so that air is directed out of the nose.
Listen to recording 46 *(https://www.bloomsburyonlineresources.com/the-accent-handbook)*.

Nasals + plosives:
Velar Nasal + Voiceless Velar Plosive (K):
Soft palate meets the middle of the tongue body so that air is directed out of the nose. The soft palate and tongue then come apart, releasing a little 'K'.
Listen to recording 47 *(https://www.bloomsburyonlineresources.com/the-accent-handbook)*.

Velar Nasal + Voiced Velar Plosive (G):
Soft palate meets the middle of the tongue body so that air is directed out of the nose. The soft palate and tongue then come apart, releasing a little 'G'.
Listen to recording 48 *(https://www.bloomsburyonlineresources.com/the-accent-handbook)*.

Doing NG

These exercises are to help you practise the accent's NG sound/s:

Exercise: **Silent Release NG**

To help make a velar nasal NG
You need: some text

Let your tongue rest in your mouth. Remind yourself of where the middle of the tongue body is and allow this part to touch the soft palate. Hum through this shape, then continue making sound but let the lips part. To check that you're making a nasal sound, pinch your nose. If the sound stops, your tongue and soft palate are in the right place.

Say the word 'sing'. When you get to the NG, bring the tongue and soft palate together and lengthen the sound. Try it again but this time make the NG shorter.

If you find that when you end the word you release a little K or a G after it, try the exercise again, say the word 'sing' and then, leaving the articulators exactly where they are, stop making sound before releasing the articulators. This way the release will be silent. Try this a few times to practise. Say the phrase with the NGs:

The king was dancing and singing all night long.

If this is a sound in the accent, add it into your text.

Exercise: **Special K**

To help make a velar nasal + K
You need: some text

Let the tongue rest in the mouth. Remind yourself of where the middle of the tongue body is and slowly raise this part to the soft palate. Hum through this shape, then continue making sound but let the lips part. To check that you're making a nasal sound, pinch your nose. If the sound stops, your tongue and soft palate are in the right place.

Say the word 'sing'. When you get to the NG, bring the tongue and soft palate together and lengthen the sound. Try it again but this time make the NG shorter. Release the tongue and soft palate so that a little 'K' escapes.

Another way to find this sound is to say the word 'think'. Say the words 'every' and 'think'. Put the two together to say 'everythink'.

You've said the word 'everything' with a special K sound! If this is a sound in the accent, add it into the text. To remind yourself of this special K NG, you could write a K in your script, for instance: 'working' can be written as 'workingk'.

Exercise: **G Thang**

To help make a velar nasal + G
You need: some text

Let the tongue rest in the mouth. Remind yourself of where the middle of the tongue body is and slowly raise this part to the soft palate. Hum through this shape, then continue making sound but let the lips part. To check that you're making a nasal sound, pinch your nose. If the sound stops, your tongue and soft palate are in the right place.

Say the word 'sing'. When you get to the NG, bring the tongue and soft palate together and lengthen the sound. Try it again but this time make the NG shorter. Release the tongue and soft palate so that a little 'G' escapes. It may sound like a little 'GUH'. If this is a sound in the accent, add it into the text.

Exercise: **Cuttin' It**

To help make an alveolar nasal
You need: some text

This sound usually only appears at the ends of words of more than one syllable. You would not usually hear it in the word 'sing', but you may hear it at the end of the word 'singing', for instance.

Start by saying the word 'in'. Take the words 'sing' and 'in'. Say them separately and then put them together to create 'singin'. Add this 'in' sound to the end of the following words:

work
laugh
play
talk

You've made the words: workin', laughin', playin', talkin'. If this is a sound in the accent, add it into the text.

Exercise: **Practising Helps NG Sounds Singgg**

To practise making the NG sounds you've noticed

Take the NGs you've noticed and practise making them in a variety of situations:

NG on its own	e.g.	NG
NG – vowel	e.g.	NGa
Vowel – NG	e.g.	eNG
Vowel-NG-vowel	e.g.	iNGu
In a word	e.g.	riNGer
In a phrase	e.g.	The king was dancing and singing all night long

If you're finding it difficult, make the sound in slow motion before gradually speeding up.

Yod

The yod is the name of one consonant sound which is only ever pronounced in one way. The sound isn't represented by one letter alone, though in some accents of English it can be pronounced when a Y or a U is written. For example:

yes   **y**ou   **u**se

Some accents of English make the yod between certain consonants and vowels such as these:

He k**new** the com**pu**ter **lu**red **su**itable **cu**te **new**ts.

In some accents of English, the yod influences certain consonant and vowel combinations so they are 'smooshed' in places such as these:

Di**d y**ou know the s**tu**pid **du**ke ate **tu**na?

The yod can be key if the new accent:

- makes the yod more or less than you = **Yod Number**
- influences the sounds around it more or less than you = **Yod Smooshing**

If the accent behaves in the same way as yours, move on to another sound.

Discovering yod

These exercises are to help work out when and how the accent uses a yod. If you already know what the accent does with yods, head to the 'Doing Yod' section for practice.

Exercise: **Make a Yod**

To help make a yod sound
If you're unsure of how a yod sounds and feels, try this exercise.

Let the tongue rest in your mouth, with the tongue tip behind your bottom front teeth. Make an AH sound. As you make this sound, raise the front of the tongue body up to the hard palate, keeping the tip where it is. Your tongue is creating a hump. As the front of the tongue body gets closer to the hard palate the sound will start to change. Move the front of the tongue body so close to the hard palate that you create a fricative sound. Release it down a little so that the 'hissing' sound stops but the tongue is still creating a hump. Drop the tongue down. Repeat this a few times, aiming to find a 'yuh' quality. Add it into the word 'YoYo'.

Another approach is to place your thumb on the hard palate. Make an AH sound and then arch the front of your tongue body up to meet your thumb and press into it. Keep the tongue tip behind the bottom front teeth.

Continue the sound and pull your thumb out of your mouth. Keep the tongue 'humped' in this position so the sound travels over the top of it. Make this sound and then drop the tongue down. Repeat this action a few times – you're making the yod! Add this sound to the beginning of the words 'yesterday', 'you' and 'yoghurt'.

Exercise: **Yodding Along**

*To explore your **Yod Number***

Try **Make a Yod** first to feel the sound in your mouth. Then say the following words in your own accent:

yes

you

yoghurt

Do you make the yod sound at the start of these words? If you're unsure, lengthen the initial sound to help focus on it. Say the following words:

music

few

cute

beauty

Do you make a yod sound between the consonants and vowels in bold in any of these words? Say the words slowly to focus on the shift from one sound to the next. Notice any resistance to the airflow between the consonant and vowel.

If you move straight from the consonant to the vowel (e.g. **m** to **u**), you aren't making a yod. If you notice some resistance, however small, between the consonant and the vowel (e.g. **m** to **y** to **u**), then you're making the yod. Say the following words:

new

pur**su**it

en**thu**se

lute

suit

Do you make a yod sound between the consonants and vowels in bold in any of these words? Say the words slowly to focus on the shifts from one sound to the next. As before, notice any resistance to the airflow between the consonant and vowel. Note down whether or not you make the yod in each of the words above.

Exercise: **Yod, Drop or Smoosh?**

To help explore how you say certain consonant and vowel combinations
Depending on the consonant and vowel combinations, accents can:

- make the yod
- not make the yod

- smoosh the sounds with the yod
- smoosh the sounds without the yod

Di**d y**ou know the st**u**pid **du**ke ate **tu**na?

Say the phrase in your own accent and notice what happens to the bits in bold. Feel the sounds in your mouth as you make them. Slow them down to focus on them. Would you best describe what you're doing for 'stupid' as:

- STYOOPID   (saying the yod)
- STOOPID   (not saying the yod)
- SHCHYOOPID   (smooshing with the yod)
- SHCHOOPID   (smooshing without the yod)

Do you do the same thing for 'did you', 'duke' and 'tuna'? Note down any discoveries.

Exercise: **Where in the Word for Yod?**

*To help explore the accent's **Yod Number***
You need: an accent recording, something to write with and on
Yod sounds can appear in different places in different accents. If you're unsure what a yod is, head to **Make a Yod** first. Play the accent recording and listen first for words that start with Y:

you, **y**ard, **y**es

Do you hear a yod at the start of words like these? Play the recording again, this time listening for any words that contain the letters B, M, F, V and C followed by 'U/OO/EW' sounds:

beauty, **mu**sic, con**fu**se, **vie**w, **cu**te

Do you hear a yod between the consonants and vowels in bold in any words like these? Play the recording once more, this time listening out for any words that contain the letters T, D, N, TH, L, S followed by 'U/OO/EW' sounds:

tune, **du**ty, **ne**w, en**thu**se, **lu**te, **su**it

Do you hear a yod between the consonants and vowels in bold in any words like these? Note your discoveries.

Exercise: **Do They Smoosh?**

To help explore how the accent pronounces certain consonant + vowel combinations
You need: an accent recording
If you have a recording of the phrase below, play it.

Di**d y**ou know the st**u**pid **du**ke ate **tu**na?

If you don't, listen to another accent recording and listen out for any of the following words:

tune, tuna
stupid
due, dew, soldier
nature, nurture, future
issue, tissue
educate
assume

Of course, your recording may not have any of these words, but if it does listen to them again and ask yourself whether you hear:

* consonant + yod + vowel (TYOONA)
* consonant + vowel (TOONA)
* smooshed consonant + yod + vowel (CHYOONA)
* smooshed consonant + vowel (CHOONA)

Note any discoveries.

Speech Bubble

The yod is a **Voiced Palatal Approximant.** The tongue tip stays behind the front bottom teeth. The front of the tongue body raises up towards the hard palate but doesn't quite touch it.

Common yod behaviours:

Pronounced:
Listen to recording 49 *(https://www.bloomsburyonlineresources.com/the-accent-handbook)*.

* you, menu, volume, continue
* tune, duty, new, lieu, enthuse, suit, lute
* beauty, music, few, view, cute

Not Pronounced:
Listen to recording 50 *(https://www.bloomsburyonlineresources.com/the-accent-handbook)*.

* tune, duty, new, lieu, enthuse, suit, lute
* beauty, music, few, view, cute

Smooshed:
The yod changes the pronunciation of the consonants surrounding it. This is also known as 'crunching' or 'coalescence'.

Listen to recording 51 *(https://www.bloomsburyonlineresources.com/the-accent-handbook)*.

- tune, duty, tissue

i.e. tune – CHOON or CHYOON

This isn't an exhaustive list of possibilities. If the accent you're learning doesn't seem to follow these behaviours, explore what is happening using the exercises in **Discovering Yod**.

Doing yod

These exercises are to help you practice the accent's yod sound/s:

Exercise: **You Beauty!**

To help insert the yod
You need: some text, a mirror (optional)
This can help if you don't make yod sounds after certain consonants, but the accent does. If you're unsure how a yod is made, go to **Make a Yod** first. In front of a mirror, practise saying it after the following sounds, pointing at your reflection to ensure the YOO (or, 'you') part is added in:

T   (T + YOO)
D   (D + YOO)
N   (N + YOO)

Work slowly at first before gradually speeding up. Add these sounds into the words:

Tune
Duty
New

It may help to rewrite these words, like: tyoon, dyooty, nyoo. If this is a sound in the accent, practise adding it into your text.

Exercise: **Fine Tooning**

To help remove the yod
You need: some text
This can help if you say the 'yuh' sound in words like 'tune' and 'duty', but the accent doesn't.

Rewriting words that contain a yod in your own accent but not in the new accent can be a useful way to remember pronunciation. Take the words:

Tune
Duty
Student

and say them:

Toon
Dooty
Stoodent

Notice how these words feel in your mouth. How would you describe them? Take the words:

Tuesday
due
new
stupid
assume
suit
lieu

Find where a yod could be removed. Say the consonant, pause and then say the vowel. Gradually speed up until the sounds are close together. It may help to think of this as an entirely new word. If the accent drops yods, practise dropping them in your text.

Exercise: **Smoosh It**

To help smoosh sounds
You need: some text
This can help if the accent smooshes sounds and you don't. Smooshing can happen in the following consonant + vowel combinations:

T + U/OO/EW
D +U/OO/EW
S +U/OO/EW

- For words with T + U/OO/EW, say them with a CH. Tune is said CHOON, or CHYOON
- For words with D +U/OO/EW, say them as J in 'juice'. Duty is said JOOTY or JYOOTY
- For words with S +U/OO/EW, say them as SH. Assume is said ASHOOM or ASHYOOM

If it helps, as you say the smooshed sounds, rub your hands together as if squishing the sounds together. If the accent smooshes sounds, find the words in your text and smoosh away! It can help to rewrite the words so that they look more similar to how you pronounce them.

Consonant clusters

Clusters are easy to see on a page. Look out for two or more consonant sounds that appear next to each other without a vowel in between:

> It's a **str**uggle to **str**oll down each **str**eet in this di**str**ict.

> The **dr**iver **dr**ove the **tr**ain along **tr**icky **tr**acks **dr**enched in **dr**oplets.

Discovering clusters

Exercise: **Catching the Clusters**

To compare how you and the new accent pronounce consonant clusters
You need: an accent recording

To find out if consonant clusters are an important feature in the new accent, check how you say them first. Say the following phrase in your own accent, as if you were delivering them as lines to someone:

> It's a **str**uggle to **str**oll down each **str**eet in this di**str**ict.

What's the overriding sound you use to make the STR cluster? Is the first sound an S or more of an SH sound? Is the R the most dominant sound? Say it again to check. Be cluster curious.

Are you making the R sound with your tongue alone or are you also using your lips to make a slight W sound? Say it again and look in a mirror to check.

Play the accent recording. Does the speaker do the same as you or are they doing something different? Take the phrase:

> The **dr**iver **dr**ove the **tr**ain along **tr**icky **tr**acks **dr**enched in **dr**oplets.

How do you make the 'T' in the word 'train'? Is it a T, CH or SH?

Listen to your speaker. Do they do the same as you or are they doing something different? What are they doing?

Speech Bubble

Common cluster types:

- Every consonant is pronounced: street – S + T + R EET
- Sounds are smooshed: street – SHTREET
- One consonant disappears: best – BES

Listen to recording 52 *(https://www.bloomsburyonlineresources.com/the-accent-handbook)*.

This isn't an exhaustive list of possibilities. These are examples of some of the more common pronunciations in accents of English.

If the accent you're learning doesn't seem to make any of these, explore what is happening using the exercises in **Discovering Clusters**.

Doing clusters

Exercise: **Step by Step**

To help make each consonant in the cluster
Inspired by the work of Barbara Houseman
You need: some text, a highlighter

If the accent you're learning pronounces all the sounds in their consonant clusters in a way that you don't, try this exercise.

Find a space with room to move. Imagine the floor is a deep river. Across the river are three stepping-stones. Each stepping-stone represents a different consonant in the cluster STR. The first is S, the second T and the final step is R, along with the rest of the word. Working with the consonant cluster words: **str**ut, **str**oll, **str**eet, cross the river, landing on each stepping-stone and saying each consonant sound.

It might look something like this:

S --- T --- RUT

Step slowly at first. You don't have to land heavily on the stones. Try the next two words, 'stroll' and 'street' using the same set of steps.

Say these words again and speed up the steps slightly, landing lightly on each stone. When you feel confident, further increase your speed.

Without the stepping-stones, say the word, checking you hit all the consonant sounds. If this happens in the accent you're learning, go through your text and highlight any clusters you see. Practise the sounds 'step by step'.

Exercise: **Take the Edge Off**

To help remove certain sounds in consonant clusters
You need: some text

This can help if the accent you're learning doesn't pronounce one or more of the sounds in a cluster, but you do. Take the following clusters:

ST as in be**st**
ND as in la**nd**
CT/KT as in impa**ct** or attac**ked**
SP as in cla**sp**

Say the words, making a gesture for the consonant you want to drop when you say it. Give it level 10 commitment. Say the words again and this time make the gesture but don't say the sound. Allow the gesture to represent it. It may also help to physically cross out the consonant/s in your text to remind you not to say them.

Exercise: **Cluster Crusher**

To help smoosh clusters

This can help if the accent you're learning smooshes sounds in consonant clusters together and you don't. Take the following clusters:

STR as in **str**ing
TR as in **tr**im
DR as in **dr**aw

Say the words slowly, tracking the journey of your tongue. Say the words again but this time imagine that your tongue is really heavy. It goes to make the S sound in 'string' but it doesn't quite make it. Instead, it moves to 'SH'.

string – SHTRING

Try doing the same for:

trim – CHTRIM
draw – JRAW

Look through your text. If you have any clusters that could be smooshed, practise them with a heavy tongue.

Other consonants

TL, DL

Ts and Ds followed by Ls can be seen in the following words:

> They gen**tl**y cra**dl**ed the li**ttl**e baby in the mi**ddl**e of the hospi**tal**.

When a T or a D is followed by an L in the spelling, it can be pronounced in a variety of ways.

Exercise: **Toodaloo!**

To explore how you make a T or D + L

> They gen**tl**y cra**dl**ed the li**ttl**e baby in the mi**ddl**e of the hospi**tal**.

Say the phrase and notice how you pronounce the T + Ls and D + Ls. If you're unsure, say the phrase slowly and pay particular attention to how you make the T and Ds. You may:

- glottal some or all of the Ts
- say the Ts or Ds and then the Ls
- create a little explosion out of the sides of the mouth between the T or D and the L. Listen to recording 53 *(https://www.bloomsburyonlineresources.com/the-accent -handbook)* for examples.

If you created a little explosion out of the sides, you made a **lateral release**. This sound appears in various accents and can be useful to learn.

Exercise: **Out the Sides!**

To help make a lateral release
You need: an accent recording, some text

Release the tongue and bring the tip or blade up to the gum ridge. Bring the sides of the tongue up to the top side teeth and breathe in and out through the mouth. Can you feel the cold air rush over the sides of the tongue when you breathe in? What does this sound like? Can you make the sound 'hiss'?

Keeping your tongue in this position, make some plosive sounds out of the sides of the mouth. You will need the tip or blade of the tongue to remain firmly on the gum ridge for this.

Say the word 'little'. Bring the tip or blade of the tongue up to the gum ridge for the T and release the air out of the sides of the mouth for the remainder of the word. Does this sound like a completely new word to you? Add this sound into the phrase:

> They gen**tl**y cra**dl**ed the li**ttl**e baby in the mi**ddl**e of the hospi**tal**.

Listen to the accent recording. Do you hear this lateral release sound? If so, add it into your text when a word has a T or D followed by an L in the spelling.

TN, DN

Ts and Ds followed by Ns can be seen in the following words:

The kit**ten** had hid**den** but**ton**s in the gar**den**.

When a T or a D is followed by an N in the spelling, it can be pronounced in a variety of ways.

Exercise: **How Do You TN DN?**

To explore how you make a T or D + N

The kit**ten** had hid**den** but**ton**s in the gar**den**.

Say the phrase and notice how you pronounce the T + Ns and D + Ns. If you're unsure, say the phrase slowly and pay particular attention to how you release the T or D. You may:

- glottal some or all of the Ts
- say the Ts or Ds and then the Ns
- create a little 'explosion' between the T or D and the N. Listen to recording 54 *(https://www.bloomsburyonlineresources.com/the-accent-handbook)* for examples.

If you created a little explosion, you made a **nasal release**. This sound appears in various accents and can be useful to learn.

Exercise: **Out the Nose!**

To help make a nasal release
You need: an accent recording, some text
Release the tongue and bring the tip or blade up to the gum ridge. Breathe through the nose with it there. As if imitating a sneeze, breathe in, keep the tongue where it is and then create a plosive out of the nose on the out-breath. Can you feel a puff of air exit the nose? Place your hand under your nose and repeat the action.

Say the word 'kitten'. Bring the tip or blade of the tongue up to the gum ridge for the T and release the air out of the nose for the remainder of the word. Does this sound like a completely new word to you? Add this sound into the phrase:

The kit**ten** had hid**den** but**ton**s in the gar**den**.

Listen to the accent recording. Do you hear this nasal release? If so, add it into your text when a word has a T or D followed by an N in the spelling.

Consonant voicing

In some accents, the following consonants often sound the same:

P and B
F and V
T and D
C/K and G
S and Z
TH in 'breath' and TH in 'breathe'

Either they are both voiced, or both voiceless. In other accents, one is usually voiceless and the other is usually voiced. Sometimes, whether they are voiced or not depends on where the consonant is in the word.

Exercise: **Am I Voicing?**

To help discover which consonants you voice in your own accent
Say the following words:

peace	**k**iss
before	**g**ood
first	**s**un
visit	**z**ebra
tonight	**th**ank
dog	**th**is

Put your fingers gently on the front of your neck and notice whether you feel vibrations when you say the first consonant sound in each word (in bold). If you're unsure, say them slowly and lengthen the sound when possible. Be careful not to mistake the consonants for the vowels that follow them, as vowels always have vibrations. Focus on the first consonant sound only.

Do you feel a vibration for all of them, none of them or some of them? Say the following words:

pul**p**	**d**ee**d**
bul**b**	**c**a**k**e
faf**f**	**g**oo**g**le
ver**v**e	**z**oo**s**
tar**t**	

Put your fingers gently on the front of your neck and notice whether you feel vibrations when you say the two bold consonant sounds in each word. If you're unsure, say them slowly and lengthen them if possible.

Do you say the two consonants in bold in exactly the same way? Do you voice every single consonant? Are all your sounds voiceless? Do you voice some and not others? Note down any discoveries.

Exercise: **To Voice or Not to Voice?**

To help notice and practise voiced and voiceless consonants in the accent
You need: a recording, some text, two different coloured highlighters
Listen to your recording and write down any words your speaker says containing the following consonants:

P, B, F, V, T, D, TH, S, Z

Listen again, this time focusing on the words you've written down. Each time you hear a word, pause the recording and mimic it as closely as you can. Did you voice the consonant in question? If you're not sure, put your fingers gently on the front of your neck and repeat the word. Did you feel vibrations on that sound?

Highlight your text using one colour for the consonants your speaker voices, and the other colour for the consonants they don't voice.

Stand in front of a wall. Read the text in the accent as best you can. When you get to a voiced consonant, push against the wall as you say it and voice the sound. When you get to a voiceless consonant, lightly touch the wall as you make the voiceless sound.

Move away from the wall and read the text again, using the highlights to remind you of the voiced and voiceless consonants.

Exercise: **Consonant Story**

To build a 'get in phrase' using the key consonants of the accent
You need: something to write with and on
Choose three consonants sounds that you consider important for the accent. Write them down and then build a sentence using words which contain these sounds. For example, you could choose R, L, yod. The phrase could be:

You always read letters while listening to tuneful music playing on the new radio.

Say the phrase in the accent. Focus on creating the consonants. You can also layer your practice by focusing on one consonant sound at a time and building up. Say the phrase a few times to hone the sounds. This could be a useful reminder to help you 'get in' to the accent.

Vowel sounds

This section looks at ways of noticing, imitating and remembering the key vowel sounds of an accent.

Remember: You can pick and choose which exercises to do. They don't have to be completed in any particular order.

Discovering vowels

Exercise: **Vowel Song**

To help explore different vowel pronunciations from your own
This exercise can be helpful if you're new to exploring vowels, or you want to practise breaking free from your habitual sounds. Take the song 'Heads, Shoulders, Knees and Toes':

> Head, shoulders, knees and toes
> Knees and toes
> Head, shoulders, knees and toes
> Knees and toes
> And eyes and ears and mouth and nose
> Head, shoulders, knees and toes
> Knees and toes

Choose a vowel sound. It could be 'OO', 'EE', 'AH' or any other. Challenge yourself to sing the entire song using that one vowel sound in each word (except for 'and'). For example, if you choose 'OO', the start of the song will go like this:

> Hood, shoolders, noos and toos,
> Noos and toos

Once you've sung the song all the way through with one vowel sound, choose a different vowel and repeat the exercise. Do this with a few different vowel sounds to free yourself up before exploring the vowels of the accent you're learning.

Exercise: **First Impression Vowels**

To help notice and shortlist key vowel sounds of the accent
You need: an accent recording, something to write with and on, a transcript of your recording (optional)
This can help you pick out vowel sounds to learn by using what immediately stands out to you. It's a way of shortlisting the sounds to prioritize what to focus on. This can be particularly helpful if you're short of time or are conscious of becoming overwhelmed.

Play the accent recording at least twice. Note down words or phrases which stand out to you in any way. Listen again and decide why they stand out. They could be:

- **different** from yours in some way
- vowel sounds which seem particularly **short** or **long**
- vowel sounds which make you think of **shapes**, e.g. round or flat
- vowel sounds which make you think of **directions**, e.g. front, back, up, down
- **repeated** vowel sounds, almost like a rhyme or a motif

You may have noticed words where the consonant rather than the vowel is distinctive. You can either leave these to one side for now, or head to the 'Consonants' section to explore them further.

Of the vowel sounds you noticed, highlight five which stand out to you most. Work on them first. If you noticed:

- words – look at **Slow Motion**, **Vowel Groups** or **Rhyme Time**
- lengths – look at **The Long and the Short of It** or **Vowel Movements**
- shapes or directions – look at **Vowel Movements**, **Slow Motion**, **The Matisse** or **Da Vinci Tongue**
- repetition – you may have found the same vowel in various words. Look at **Slow Motion**, **Vowel Groups** or **Vowel Clouds**.

Exercise: **Slow Motion**

To help imitate a vowel sound of the accent
You need: an accent recording
This exercise can help you hone your imitation of a vowel sound by slowing down. It can be useful if you find yourself repeating the vowel over and over, without feeling as if you're quite 'getting' it.

Choose a vowel sound from the accent to focus on. Try **First Impression Vowels** first if you need help picking one out.

Play your accent recording and listen for that vowel in a word. Pause the recording and copy the vowel as closely as you can.

Now imagine you've been slowed to a quarter of your regular speed; from the way you move your body to the way you speak. Say the vowel again in this slow-motion state.

Repeat it, focusing on your lips. Are they pouty, rounded, unrounded or spread? Say it again, focusing on your tongue. Copy the sound several times at this slowed down speed. What shape or shapes is the tongue making in the mouth?

Repeat this with other vowels of the accent. Note down any discoveries.

Exercise: **The Long and the Short of It**

To help notice and copy vowel lengths of the accent

You need: an accent recording, something to write with and on, text or script (optional)
This exercise explores vowel length, which can help with individual sounds as well as the overall rhythm of the accent.

To explore vowel length for yourself, say the word 'loose' with a long 'OO'. Now say it with the shortest 'OO' you possibly can. Switch between a long and a short 'OO'. Say the following phrase first with long OOs, then short OOs:

You move balloons to a new room.

Play the accent recording and listen out for any words which sound noticeably longer or shorter than yours. You may hear it in the overall rhythm of speech; it could sound 'smooth', or 'spiky', for instance. You may have already shortlisted some distinctive sounds using the **First Impression Vowels** exercise. If so, have the list to hand.

Play the recording again and echo any words with distinctively different vowel lengths. To feel the difference, pause the recording, echo the word, then say it again, this time in your own accent. Go back and forth between the two. Note down any discoveries.

To develop this exercise further: Take your script and read all or a section of it aloud in the accent as best you can. Are there words which need a longer or shorter vowel than your own? Mark or highlight them. Read it again and when you come to a long vowel, exaggerate the length. Add a physical gesture to help you remember it. When you come to a short vowel, add a different physical gesture.

Exercise: **Vowel Movements**

To help notice and copy vowel movements of the accent
You need: an accent recording, something to write with and on
This exercise can help you hone the shape of a vowel by exploring if it's still or moving. You may want to shortlist some vowels to look at using the **First Impression Vowels** exercise first.

Still vowels (also known as monophthongs) mean the lips and tongue body stay in one position for the entirety of the sound. **Moving** vowels (also known as diphthongs and triphthongs) mean the lips and tongue body start in one position then move to a second or even third position within one syllable.

To experience this for yourself, put your lips and tongue in a position of your choice and make a vowel sound. Lengthen it without moving your lips and tongue. This is a **still** vowel. Put your lips and tongue in a different position and make another still vowel.

Make the first vowel again, followed by the second. Now slowly glide from the first into the second. Make the move gradual at first, then speed up. Can you move from the first to the second within one syllable? This is an example of a **moving** vowel.

Choose a vowel sound from the accent to focus on. Play your accent recording and listen for that sound in a word. When you hear it, pause the recording, rewind and listen to it a few times. Echo what you hear. Do it with your eyes closed, focusing on your mouth as it shapes the sound. Do you feel any movement? Decide whether you think that vowel is still or moving.

Repeat this with other key vowels of the accent. Note down any discoveries.

Exercise: **Make a Move**

To help shape a moving vowel of the accent
You need: an accent recording

This exercise helps you make moving vowels (also known as diphthongs and triphthongs). It can be helpful if you're struggling to make one or more parts of the sound.

Choose a moving vowel of the accent you're learning. Find a space with room to move. Play your accent recording if you need a reminder of the vowel. Say the start of the vowel only, positioning your lips and tongue body to make the sound. Stop.

Move to another part of the space and make the next part of the vowel, positioning your lips and tongue body accordingly. If you have chosen a moving vowel with three different sounds (a triphthong), move to another part of the space and make the final sound.

Repeat this. Start in one place with the beginning of the vowel, stop and move to a different space for the second part (and then the third if applicable). Do you feel the difference in shape for each part of the vowel?

Do this once more, making the transition from one position to another a little faster. Then, stand still and use your hand to represent the journey from one position to another.

Put the vowel into words, keeping a sense of the movement from one position to another. Mark up your text or script to remind yourself of this moving vowel.

Exercise: **Vowel Groups**

To help group and remember vowels of the accent
You need: an accent recording, something to write with and on

When learning the vowel sounds of an accent, it can be difficult to know which sound goes in which word. This exercise offers a way of grouping vowels to help you remember and reproduce them. These groups can be especially helpful when applying an accent to a script.

The groups were devised by phonetician J. C. Wells and you might hear them referred to as **lexical sets**.

Look at the list on page 146. Each group heading (in capital letters) represents a different vowel group. No matter the accent, every word in a particular group will likely be pronounced using the same vowel sound. For instance, if you know how the new accent pronounces the vowel in 'DRESS', you can predict that other words in that group (step, deaf, said) will have the same vowel sound.

Group Heading	Example words/spellings:
KIT	ship, myth, busy, pretty, guilt, women, sieve
DRESS	step, deaf, any, friend, said, bury
TRAP	tap, hand, plaid, cat
LOT	stop, watch, quality, knowledge
STRUT	cup, won, touch, blood
FOOT	put, good, look, could, woman
BATH	staff, class, laugh, can't
CLOTH	gone, cough, sausage, wash
NURSE	hurt, work, bird, term, earth, journal
FLEECE	meet, these, brief, ceiling, meat, people, ski
FACE	tape, wait, play, they, rein, weigh, great
PALM	calm, father, bra, spa, lager
THOUGHT	taught, fought, sauce, jaw, fall, water, broad
GOAT	road, both, toe, own, dough, sew
GOAL	old, soul, coal, mole, bowl
GOOSE	loop, who, move, you, rude, few, juice, beauty
PRICE	ripe, type, sign, buy, height
CHOICE	join, toy, royal
MOUTH	out, down, plough
NEAR	fear, beer, here, pier, hero, weird
SQUARE	care, fair, pear, where, their, vary, aerial
START	far, scarf, heart
NORTH	for, war, quarter, aura
FORCE	four, wore, soar, door, source
CURE	poor, tour, pure, curious, Europe
happY	copy, taxi, coffee, money, Chelsea
lettER	paper, metre, sugar, major, succour, martyr, figure
commA	visa, saga, dementia

Slowly read the group names and the example words in your **own accent**. Notice the sounds of the vowels in each line. The words in each line may sound as though they half-rhyme as you're using the same vowel. Note: If English isn't your first language, it might not be helpful to read the vowel groups in your own accent of English first. This is because you may not have a habitual way of saying certain vowel sounds in English. If this is the case, you may find it helpful to move on to the next stage of this exercise.

You might notice that you use the same vowel sound in a few groups, for example **NORTH** and **FORCE**. If this is the case, you **merge** these two groups in your accent.

You might notice that you use more than one sound in a group, for example **NURSE** 'hurt, work, bird, term'. This doesn't happen a lot, but if you notice it then you **split** the NURSE group in your accent. This is useful to know, as the accent you are learning may do something different.

Play your accent recording. When you hear a word with a different vowel sound from your own, pause the recording.

Working in your **own accent**, say the word and then the first in the list of vowel groups (KIT). Does the vowel sound the same? If it does, the chances are it lives in this group. If it doesn't, say your word again and then say the second word in the list. Does it sound the same? Work your way down the list until you find the word with the same vowel sound. For example, say the word was 'tea':

tea – KIT
tea – DRESS
tea – TRAP
tea – LOT (No luck so far . . .)
tea – STRUT
tea – FOOT
tea – BATH
tea – CLOTH
tea – NURSE
tea – FLEECE (The same vowel!)

If you find more than one group for your word, use the Vowel Spelling Guide on p. 189 to help you categorize it.

Once you've worked out which vowel group it is in, try **Slow Motion, The Long and the Short of It** and **Vowel Movements** to work out how this sound is made. You can then apply this sound to all words in that vowel group.

Exercise: **Rhyme Time**

To help group and remember vowels of the accent
You need: an accent recording, some text or your script
It can be helpful to group and remember vowels of the accent through rhyme. For the purposes of this exercise, rhyme means a word with the same vowel sound, sometimes making it more of a 'half-rhyme'. For instance, 'hot', 'lot', 'stop', 'sock' and 'lob' are all considered to rhyme in this exercise.

If you've already shortlisted some key vowels, have your list to hand. Otherwise, play the accent recording and pause when you hear a different vowel sound from your own.

Say the word in the accent as best you can. It does not need to sound perfect. Now say another word in the accent which rhymes with that word. For example, the word you picked out is 'gave'. You could then say, 'save' or 'brave' and you also could say, 'gain', 'day', 'aid' and so on. Lengthen the words to give yourself time to hear and feel the vowel you're making.

Continue adding words to the list. How many can you think of? By doing this you'll get used to saying the new vowel sound and putting it into words. The more familiar you get with this, the easier it may be to remember it, and to find the sound again when you come to read a script.

Note down the sound to help you remember it in any way that works for you. You could make the rhyming words into a memorable phrase, for example.

Exercise: **Vowel Clouds**

To help divide merged vowel groups of the accent
You need: something to write with and on
This can be helpful if the accent you're learning uses two vowel pronunciations where you would only use one. For example, you say 'mast' and 'mat' using the same vowel sound, but you've heard the accent using two different vowels for these two words.

Pick two words you would pronounce with the same vowel sound, but the accent would say with two different vowels. Write each word on a separate piece of paper. These are your two vowel clouds.

Take a third piece of paper and write down as many words as you can think of which have the same vowel as those first two in your own accent. For example, say you've written 'mast' and 'mat' because you say them with the same vowel. You could write words like: 'past', 'pat', 'cat', 'after' and so on.

Go to the Vowel Spelling Guide on p. 189 to help you work out which words on this list are in which cloud. Alternatively, if you can, ask someone with the accent to read your list of words to help you decide which cloud they live in.

As you work out which cloud a word lives in, write it on one of the two vowel clouds. Pin your word clouds up. Whenever you think of another word that's in either of the groups, work out which cloud it lives in and add it. These vowel clouds can be handy references when you are applying the accent to a script.

Doing vowels

The following exercises can help you to refine and take ownership of the vowel sounds you've discovered and help embed them in your memory.

Exercise: **The Matisse**

To help take ownership of the accent's vowel sounds
You need: an accent recording, something to write with and on
This exercise can be useful if you find yourself struggling to make a vowel sound.

Choose a vowel sound from the accent to explore. Play the accent recording, listening for this sound. Imitate the sound by echoing the words you hear it in. Try not to worry if your imitation doesn't sound accurate to you. Just copy as best you can.

Listen again. As you imitate the sound, use your arm to draw it in the air in a way that makes sense to you. Listen once more and as you imitate, draw the sound on a page. Stop the recording and, using your arm movement or drawing as a reminder, make the sound again. Put the sound into some words. Make up a short phrase using those words.

Repeat this with other key vowels to build a physical and visual relationship with the sound and make it more memorable.

Exercise: **Vowel Story**

To build a 'get in phrase' using the vowels of the accent
You need: something to write with and on
Once you've gained a sense of the key vowel sounds of the accent, you can build a memorable phrase with them to help you 'get in' to the accent.

Choose five different vowels to play with and write down five words, each containing one of the different vowels. Alternatively, you could use the vowel group headings from the **Vowel Groups** exercise. Make these words into a phrase. For example, you could choose: 'cup', 'past', 'team', 'like', 'take'. The phrase could be:

Take the **cup** you **like past** the **team**.

Say the phrase in the accent as best you can. Say it a few times to hone the vowel sounds. This could be a useful 'get in' phrase for the accent.

Exercise: **Moving the Story**

To physicalize the vowels of the accent
You need: some text
Take the phrase you created in **Vowel Story** and generate a physical action for each of the key words. Give a different action to each vowel group. You can use your whole body to create an action, or just one body part.

Say your phrase in the accent with the different actions. Do it a few times so that you begin to embed the movements.

Read a piece of text in the accent as best you can. When you get to a word that you recognize as being in one of the vowel groups from **Vowel Story**, do the movement. This can help to embed the vowel sounds into your muscle memory.

Exercise: **Slang Dictionary**

To gain confidence with the accent's vowel sounds
You need: something to write with and on
This exercise can help you take ownership of the vowels of the new accent.

Make a shortlist of the vowel sounds you feel are most important for the accent. Pick one to play with.

Start by saying the vowel on its own a few times, getting used to the feel and sound of it. Put it into a word. Write the word down. Put it into two or three more words and write them down. Try to use words with the sound in different places (first syllable e.g. **hec**tic, second syllable e.g. coll**ect**.)

Once you have three or four different words with the same vowel sound written down, say them out loud. They might seem like they rhyme or half-rhyme.

You're going to turn this into your own 'slang' for the accent. Say the words again and make up a meaning for them. For example, your words could be 'utter' and 'gut', which you could pretend was slang in the accent for being hungry: 'I am utter gut'!

Repeat this with the other vowel sounds on your shortlist until you've created a little slang dictionary for yourself. You can use this rhyming slang as part of your 'short-hand' for getting into the accent.

Exercise: **Da Vinci Tongue**

To help hone the accent's vowels by focusing on the tongue
You need: an accent recording, modelling clay/dough/plasticine
This exercise can help give you a sense of what your tongue body is doing to make vowels. It might help to do the **Tongue Animation** exercise on p. 81 first.

Using some mouldable material like modelling clay, dough or plasticine, make a model of a tongue, copying one of the images on pp. 23–24. Remind yourself of the different parts. Spend some time moving your model tongue about. How many different positions can you mould it into?

Each time you create a position, see if you can recreate it with your actual tongue. You may be surprised at how many you're able to copy.

Make a vowel sound of your choosing. Work out what your tongue is doing and mould the model tongue to copy the shape. If you can't tell what your tongue is doing, look in the mirror or feel it with your finger. If you have chosen a moving vowel, make the different parts of the sound and mould the model tongue accordingly.

Play the accent recording. When you hear a vowel sound that differs from yours, pause the recording and copy it as best you can. Lengthen the sound to get a better sense of what your tongue is doing and mould your model tongue into the same shape.

Make the vowel sound again with your actual tongue. How does it sound? Check it using the accent recording. If it doesn't sound quite right, make any adjustments to your actual tongue and your model tongue to copy the sound as closely as you can.

Repeat this with other vowels of the accent. Note down any discoveries or mark up your script so you can remember the vowels later.

Exercise: **Faux-netics**

To help remember the accent's vowels when reading text
Sometimes, it can be hard to remember the new vowels of the accent when you come to read text. This is because our brains are often wired to see spelling on a page and automatically use our habitual sounds. Take this vowel sentence:

The stock pot is hot.

In your own accent, when you see an 'o' in a word you might automatically want to round your lips. However, in another accent, this sound may need to be made with unrounded lips. A way around this is to rewrite words in the sentence in a way that makes sense for you:

The **stahk paht** is **haht.**

When your eyes see the 'ah', your lips might now release and make the right shape for the sound. Try this yourself using vowels you find tricky and rewrite your text!

Part C   Acting

Part C is about **performing in the accent**. It offers various ways of approaching:

- Accent and script
- Accent and character
- Accent and situation
  - for the character
  - for the actor

Accent and dialect work is often undertaken by the actor alone, without a dialect coach to help. It might be fitted in *around* rehearsals or filming and this may cause a separation. The accent can seem like an afterthought, 'pasted on', or it can completely dominate a performance and take you out of that moment-by-moment connection.

Part C can help connect your understanding of the accent with your acting process earlier, and at a deeper level. The exercises can:

- increase the chances of embedding the sounds
- improve confidence
- move accent work beyond the 'technical' and into the creative space

For help on finding an accent recording (audio or video), go to the **Listening** section on p. 33

Remember: You can pick and choose which exercises to do. They don't have to be completed in any particular order.

Go to **Part B** if:

- you want guidance on listening and finding accent examples
- you want to discover and practise an accent's features

Accent and script

Words mean more than what is set down on paper. It takes the human voice to infuse them with deeper meaning.

– Maya Angelou

Many of us lose our way when it comes to applying the sounds of the accent to the written word. It can be hard to figure out which sounds fit with which words or parts of words, let alone string them together into sentences. Equally, it can feel like the accent is taking over, or that you're losing track of what you're saying, or simply forgetting to act!

Difficulties tend to arise if you force your brain to **multitask** before it's ready. You're telling it to identify words on the page, make sense of them, read them aloud, all while using different sounds to those you would usually. That's four tasks simultaneously.

The good news is that multitasking can be built up gradually and it gets easier with time and practice. The following exercises offer various ways of building a relationship with your text and forging connections between words and sounds, layering your tasks rather than trying to do them simultaneously.

Think of it this way: if you were learning how to juggle from scratch you would start by throwing one ball and working your way up to two, three, four balls and so on. You might even start with scarves which are slower to fall so you're more likely to catch them. The same principle applies here.

Approaching text

Exercise: **First Glance**

To help make the text work for you

You need: your text, a way of marking up your text

Look at a copy of your text. This could be a digital or hard copy. How helpful does it strike you at first glance? Do the layout and font help or hinder? Is the text clear? If not, change it. If it's digital, copy and paste it into a different document, change the font, the sizing and spacing, the page colour, decorate it with doodles if it makes it look more appealing to you. If it's a hard copy, try cutting out the pages and pasting them into a book or folder with space to make notes around the sides. Making your text more 'user-friendly' can make the work ahead feel more 'friendly' too!

Exercise: **Plot It**

To help make sense of text through storytelling

You need: your text, something to write with and on (optional), a volunteer (optional)

You can do this by yourself or with a partner. Tell the story of the text, both what happens in the plot and to your character. It could be a particular monologue, a scene or the full text. You can do any of the following:

Drawing: create a cartoon or storyboard for the plot with title cards to separate scenes or moments.

Silent movie: give a silent, speedy performance of the plot, with lots of movement and even title cards.

Tableau: create a series of silent, still poses as your character, showing their journey.

Narration: give a summary of the text to yourself or a partner, as if you've just been to see the movie version. You can also narrate in the accent.

Doing any of these can help you establish a relationship with the story and your character.

Introducing accent

Try the following exercises in any order. Perhaps start with exercises that make you feel more confident. What those are will depend on the accent, the script and the project you're working on. The timing of when to introduce the accent to script is different for everyone so feel free to explore when it works best for you.

Exercise: **Scaffolding Sounds**

To help find accent sounds in text and layer your practice

You need: your text

Choose a portion of text to focus on. Pick five sounds for the accent that are important for you to remember. To help select the five sounds, you can use any of the following exercises in Part B: **Sound Shortlisting** (p. 74), **Consonant Checklist** (p. 83) and **First Impression Vowels** (p. 142). Write them down, for example:

- R
- Vowel (your own way of noting the sound)
- L
- Vowel
- T

Speak these sounds out loud as best you can in the accent. Take the first sound and read your text adding only that sound in. Other features of the accent might 'creep in' but try to stay focused on making that one sound clearly and consistently as you speak the text. It won't sound like the accent yet but you're building up.

For the second reading, add the second sound so that you're focusing on two. Do this until you've added in all five. If you find yourself forgetting sounds as you build up, don't panic! Go back and explore one sound at a time, independently of the others. Then explore two or three, until you feel confident enough to add more in.

Once you have added all five sounds in, notice how the accent sounds. Has focusing on these sounds helped other sounds fall into place too?

Exercise: **Colour Code**

To help make sound changes more visible
You need: coloured pens, pencils, stickers or highlighters, your text
Assign colours to major sounds for the new accent, for example Red = an important vowel sound, Blue = L Sound and so on.

Create a key at the front of your script or stick it on a wall or the fridge. Try to limit the number of colours to avoid the page becoming overcrowded. Then colour-code your script using the key. This will make it easier to see when the sound changes occur.

Exercise: **Mouthing Movements**

To help feel the shapes and sounds of the accent
You need: your text
Start this exercise by adopting the overall shapes of the accent you discovered in Part B and say some words or phrases.

Read your text in the shapes of the accent, silently mouthing the words. You could use the **Nonsense Passage** (p. 187) instead if you prefer. Focus your attention on how the shapes feel and the way they flow together.

Mouth the text again, focusing your attention on the accent's consonant sounds. Did you feel as though there were any tricky combinations? Underline any that stuck out to you, go back and mouth them again slowly.

Mouth the text a third time, paying attention to the vowel sounds. Notice the way you're shaping them in the mouth, and the length of them. Return to your accent recording to check any sounds you are uncertain of.

Mouth the text with a sense of your character and their intention. Notice whether this has any effect on the sounds. Finally, read the text aloud in the accent. Consider and note any discoveries.

Exercise: **Once More with Feeling**

To help blend technique and instinct
You need: your text
This exercise is one to pepper throughout your learning process. You will rarely, if ever, be asked to deliver an accent purely for accuracy purposes. It's about speaking with the voice of the character, not the voice of a general area or region. The task is to blend the features of the accent that you've observed into the line, while you speak

the intention of the character. If you're thinking about the accent, you're not thinking in character.

Select one phrase or short sentence from your script. Say the line, paying attention to the features of the accent. Do you have a sense of where the sounds of the accent are in the line and how they fit together?

Say the line again, focusing on these sounds as well as the overall shape of the accent in your mouth.

You're going to say this line 'once more with feeling'. Who are they speaking to? Where are they? Why are they saying this? What do they want? Consider these questions before you say the line to help you access the character.

Fix the listener in your line of vision (it could be a spot on the wall, or a lamp if there's no one with you). Say the line now as the character. Say it once more, really committing to the stakes of the situation.

Go back to the line and focus again on the accent, not on acting. Then go back to acting. Pivoting back and forth from technical focus to acting focus can help embed the accent features while taking ownership of the lines.

Exercise: **Fascinating Rhythm**

To avoid getting stuck in a repetitive or obvious rhythmic pattern
You need: your text, a recording device (optional)
Do you find that after some time working on the accent you get stuck in a rut with the rhythm? That it feels heavy, repetitive or that it dominates your performance? If you're not sure whether this is happening to you, record yourself saying some of your text and listen back to check.

Take one of your longer lines or sentences. Break it into smaller chunks. If there are commas in it, use them. Memorize it as much as you can so you don't have to look at the page.

Find a space with room to move. Walk around as you say your line, changing direction slightly between each little 'chunk'. Say the line again, walking at a very slow pace, almost in slow motion. Make the length of the line match the length of the sentence, again changing direction between each 'chunk'. Say it again walking at a different speed, perhaps a fast walk. Try another few speeds before saying the line standing still. Does the line feel different?

Alternatively, jog around the space until you're out of breath, then stop and say your line. Has the rhythm been disrupted? Play hopscotch or skip as you say the line, then say it again standing still. Any difference?

Place two to three objects around the room. It could be the contents of your bag or any objects already in the space. Say the line and lightly hit a different object every time you want to emphasize a word or a syllable. How many did you hit? Did the distance between them affect the rhythm of the line? Move the objects so they're spaced out differently. Repeat the exercise. Did the new arrangement affect the rhythm? Try any of the above alternatives with other lines or with longer chunks of text.

Exercise: **Unchained Melody**

To avoid getting stuck in repetitive pitch patterns
You need: your text, a recording device (optional)
If you're working on an accent with distinctive pitch patterns, it can be tempting to use these patterns in every phrase, sentence or line. This can leave the accent sounding repetitive, or as though the accent work is compromising your performance.

If you're not sure whether this is happening to you, record yourself saying some of your text and listen back to check.

Find a quiet space. Take several separate lines or sentences to play with. Read the lines on the page but instead of speaking, hum them. Make the tune different from the repetitive patterns you have been following. Then if you feel confident, sing the lines instead of speaking, making up a tune as you go. Now speak the lines. Has anything shifted or been freed up?

Exercise: **Intention Hunter**

To help find emphasis and avoid repetitive patterns
You need: your text
If you feel the accent taking over and dictating how you're saying your lines, it can help to return to the intention behind each one.

Start with one phrase or short sentence at a time. Read the phrase or sentence aloud in your own accent.

What's the one word in the phrase the listener or other characters must hear? Limit yourself to one. Say the line again in your own accent, leaning into that one word with your voice. Underline the word.

Say the phrase again, this time in the accent, leaning once more into the word you chose. You may have emphasized it slightly differently now that you're using the accent, but the intention behind the emphasis should still be true to your original intention.

Accent and character

The human voice is the organ of the soul.

– Henry Wadsworth Longfellow

Finding the way your character speaks is fundamentally a way to understand, empathize with and embody them. Consider how much the way you speak reflects your background and personality, or how you're feeling at any given moment. The following exercises provide ways of linking yourself, the accent and the character, integrating your technical work into your creative rehearsal process. They can be done in any order.

Exercise: **Stranger to Local**

To help deepen your relationship with the location of the accent
You need: access to the internet
To take on the accent of the character it's a good idea to familiarize yourself with the environment the accent was created by and exists in. Use this exercise to navigate from being an accent stranger, to tourist, to local. If you're working on a real accent within a fictional setting (fantasy, sci-fi, dystopian etc.), it may help to look at the real-world background before delving into the fictional part.

Open your browser and locate the home of the character on a world map. What continent is it in? What country? How widely is English spoken there? What other languages are spoken?

Zoom into the country. If you can, view a satellite image so you can see the real landscape. Can you see mountains, fields, water, towns, cities? Zoom further into the specific town or city, then to the neighbourhood. Zoom in to view the streets if you can. Is it rural or built up? What does it look like?

Imagine yourself as a tourist in the area. Look up local attractions and places of interest. Research the history. Is it famous for anything? Find out about local foods and traditions.

Now imagine that you're moving to the area. What is the local industry? Where are the best places to live, to shop, to eat? How do the locals spend their leisure time? What you discover here will help you refine your search for accent recordings (see exercise **Search Party** (p. 35) for further help). It could also give you clues to the character and even the accent.

Exercise: **Secret Sound**

To help connect an accent feature with character trait
You need: your text

Is there one accent feature above all others that you feel helps you most with the accent? Go through the features and pick one that you enjoy doing, or which you feel typifies the accent.

This is your character's 'secret sound'. The sound that, to you, represents a key part of their nature, or physical presence. Consider what it could be as you make the sound a few times. It could be their openness, their naivety, their determination or simply the way they plant their feet on the ground. It's up to you. Emphasize the sound to familiarize yourself with and embed it.

Try a few lines containing the sound, with the sense of this part of your character's psyche or physicality in your mind and body. Perhaps, every time you use this sound from now on, you can relish the way it roots your character.

Exercise: **Accent Backstory**

To help connect accent features memorably with story
You need: your text

Connecting imaginatively with the accent features can make them feel more secure as you build your character. Think of it like blocking: if you move a prop at some point in a scene, there must be a reason for doing so connected to the character's objective or the story. If there is no reason attached to the action, it's likely to ring false.

Pick five features for the accent that are important for you to remember. To help select the five sounds, you can use any of the following exercises in Part B: **Sound Shortlisting** (p. 74), **Consonant Checklist** (p. 83) and **First Impression Vowels** (p. 142). Write them down, for example:

- R
- Vowel (your own way of noting the sound)
- Rhythm
- Vowel
- T

Select one feature to focus on first. Create a backstory for this feature as if it, too, is a character. Why does it have its shape? Why does it sound and move the way it does? Use what you know about the setting and the plot of the piece to reinforce the backstory. You could draw a portrait of the feature or give it a symbol, so you remember its story.

Read some lines from your text with the backstory of that feature fresh in your mind. Reflect on any discoveries from this reading. Try this with the other key features.

Exercise: **Sound Personality**

To help shape and build a connection to the accent's sounds
You need: an accent recording

This can help you build a relationship with individual sounds, making them more memorable and establishing them in your muscle memory. Try this if you're struggling to imitate or remember a particular sound, especially when you're improvising or using your script.

Choose a sound to focus on. It could be a vowel or a consonant. Play your recording and listen out for that sound. Pause the recording, imitate it as best you can and ask yourself, 'What is the sound's "personality"?'

Your answer to this could be something the sound reminds you of. Say, for example, you're working on a particular R sound. It could be that, to you: 'It sounds like a pirate', 'it makes me think of Clint Eastwood' or 'it sounds like someone gargling'.

Find some space either seated or standing and make the sound, giving it a sense of the 'personality' you've chosen. You could do this through movement, facial expression or just imagining the 'personality'. Do it a few times with 100 per cent commitment. Does the sound's 'personality' connect in any way to a part of your character's personality? Their background? Their objectives?

Read some text and when you come to the sound, imitate the sound 'personality' each time. Note down any discoveries or reminders on your script or elsewhere. If, at a later stage with the accent, you find yourself losing the sense of the sound or missing it out entirely, remind yourself of its 'personality'.

Exercise: **Tasting the Sounds**

To help create a sensory connection to sound
You need: your text

Connecting your sensory memory with pronunciation can be hugely beneficial and can help create stronger links with the character and their location.

Select several accent features to play with, including one you find more challenging or less memorable.

Decide on your character's favourite food and drink. You can find ideas by looking into the cuisine of the area the accent comes from, or from any textual clues.

Match one of the sounds of the accent with one of your character's favourite tastes. Perhaps their long vowels are like the maple syrup they put on their morning pancakes, or an explosive consonant reminds you of spicy chicken. You could even have the food and drink ready to taste before or after you make the sounds if you have them available to you.

Speak some text and 'taste' the sounds as you come to them. Reflect on any discoveries you have had.

Exercise: **The Interview**

To help practise moving in and out of accent, getting closer to character
You need: two chairs (optional)
This exercise asks you to move in and out of character and accent. It can be helpful for improvising in the accent, building ways of shifting into the accent quickly, as well as aligning accent and character.

You're going to play two roles: your character and an interviewer. You could even set up two chairs and move from one to the other as you conduct the interview.

As the interviewer, ask the character a question out loud in your own accent. Answer it as your character, in their accent. If you're using two chairs, swap from one to the other before you give your answer. It's up to you how in-depth or personal this interview becomes. Keep going for at least five minutes. Reflect on any discoveries you have had.

Exercise: **I Wish I'd Said That!**

To help increase flexibility in the accent
In this exercise, use what you know about the way the character thinks to play and improvise in the accent.
Pick a character from the script that your character has a relationship to. It could be a friend, lover, family member, work colleague or anyone else they know. Improvise a scene in which your character wants something from them. It could be something emotional or physical. You can imagine their responses but keep interacting with the imaginary person.

The conversation doesn't go as smoothly as you expect it to. How does this affect how you respond in the accent? Does the rhythm vary? Do you make any of the sounds or stresses differently? Do the shapes of the accent shift? What changes and what stays in the accent?

Don't worry if the accent goes awry because you're only playing, and you can always listen to your recording again. This is an opportunity to stretch the boundaries of your character beyond what they say in the text.

Exercise: **Target Practice**

To help align accent with character objectives
You need: your text
Pick a scene or speech to play with, read it through and clarify your character's overall objective. What do they want? Keep it simple and active.

Find a space with room to move. Take one object, wall or area in the room and stand back from it. This is your target. Speaking in the accent, aim your lines at it phrase by phrase, trying to 'hit' your overall objective.

When in the line or phrase you shoot at the target is up to you. How you aim the sound at the target is also up to you, but it may help if you add a gesture such as the motion of shooting an arrow, a slingshot, throwing a javelin or even an axe. For example, take the first phrase and imagine you're aiming and shooting an arrow at the target, your objective. At what point in the phrase did you let the arrow go? On what sound? What did it do to the sound?

Keep going, phrase by phrase. When you get to the end of the scene or speech, reflect on any discoveries.

To develop this exercise further: Use some nearby objects. They could be the contents of your bag or recycling bin, ornaments, mugs or even cutlery – whatever is available to you. Place the objects in different areas around the space. You can use the objects as targets that you need to 'hit' to meet your objective. Some of them will be nearer, some further away, some big, some small. How does this affect how you say each phrase in the accent?

Exercise: **Make a Match**

To help play with opposing character and accent features

What if some of the accent features seem to contrast or conflict with the features or nature of your character? For example, you notice that the speaker you've listened to has a released and open jaw, but your character is of a tense or nervous disposition. This is quite common and there are various ways of approaching it.

Narrow down what it is about the accent that is different from your character. Is it the movement of the tongue, lips or jaw? Is it something in the patterns or the overall weight of the accent? For example, your character feels 'light' and 'floaty', but the accent feels 'heavy' and 'punchy'.

One option is to change your attitude either to the accent feature or to the character. Does the accent have to be 'punchy'? Could you change the word to 'pointy' to fit with the lightness of the character? Does the character always have to feel 'light'? Perhaps they could have heavier, punchier moments at different moments in the piece or scene? Experiment with modifying either the character trait or accent feature. Is there a point at which you've moved too far away from the core of either? Find that point and stay within it.

Another option is to switch the focus towards other features that accent and character share. Is there something else in the accent that would highlight a character feature? Go through the shapes of the tongue, lips and jaw. Do any of their movements chime with the feel of the character?

Focus on the patterns. Is there something in the rhythm you could use? Maybe the jaw of the character needs to be released for the purposes of the accent, but you could make the rhythm more rigid or fragmented to show the character's tense nature.

Perhaps a vowel or consonant sound reminds you of the character's attitude. You could try the exercise **Secret Sound** (p. 161) to help with this. Highlight where you see the sound on the page, using it to bind the character with the way they speak.

Exercise: **I Speak, Therefore I Am**

To help increase familiarity with and take ownership of the accent

This exercise can be useful if you've got to a reasonable level with the accent, but it still feels effortful to 'wear', like a new pair of shoes. The answer to this is to 'wear it in'.

Undertake a routine task such as doing your laundry, making your morning cup of coffee, or preparing a meal. As you go about the task, narrate everything you're doing in the accent. For instance, '*I am opening the fridge door and looking inside to see if I have any carrots. I am taking out the carrots and getting a knife to chop them. I am trying to decide if I want mashed or boiled potatoes*' and so on.

Repeat this exercise on different occasions and notice if you start to become more comfortable with the feel of the new accent. You can also make it more personal by narrating your inner thoughts rather than your actions. For example, '*I feel warm, I might open a window*' or '*I wonder if my package will arrive today*'.

Once you've done the exercise a few times, take time to consider what you feel like when you're speaking in the accent. What version of yourself emerges? For example: assertive, flirtatious, energetic and steadfast. Write down what you notice.

Exercise: **Swear on Your Life**

To help lower inhibitions and improve confidence in the accent
You need: your text

Swearing in an accent can be very liberating. In fact, numerous studies have shown that swearing can have many physical, social and psychological benefits.[1]

Swearing can give you a sense of control and confidence with the new accent. It's also a way of bringing humour into your work to de-escalate the stakes.

Read a section of text and add some choice expletives in and around your lines. Purely for practice purposes, of course! Choose swear words that your speaker would use. Are there some already in the script? Look up any local swear or slang words and pepper them into your foul-mouthed tirade.

Go completely off-script, using any bad language that comes into your head. Reflect on how this made you and the accent feel.

Exercise: **Grit into Gold**

To use the new or 'tricky' sound to your advantage
You need: accent recording, some text

There will, without doubt, be a sound or two that you're less confident about. One which feels 'tricky' and gets in the way, like grit on a lens. An instinct can be to rush over it to get to other, more comfortable sounds but this can mean you never really master it. One way to deal with this is to challenge your mindset by thinking of it not as grit, but as gold. That sound is the only option the character knows. That gold sound is currency which they use to express themselves and get what they want.

Play your accent recording and listen only for the challenging sound, as if searching for gold nuggets. Whenever you hear that sound, you've found another piece. Stop the recording when you feel you've collected enough. Rewind as many times as you like and enjoy listening to the gold sounds sparkling out at you. Echo the sound using the words in the recording. Say other words with this sound. Replay the recording if the sound slips.

Try some lines of your text which contain the sound. Whenever you get to the gold, use it as currency by leaning into it in whatever way suits you. You could get louder, lengthen it or change pitch, for instance.

You don't have to take the emphasis on this sound all the way through to performance, but by embracing it you will have gone a long way to establishing a familiarity which can secure it in the long run.

Accent and situation

Without context words and actions have no meaning at all.
– Gregory Bateson

This section is about using the accent in different contexts, both as an actor and as the character. Think of your own voice. You don't use it in the same way every day, in every place, in every situation, with every person. Humans are social creatures, changing the use of our bodies and voices depending on need.

Accent and situation for character
There can be a tendency to see an accent as a fixed thing but remember, you're not speaking 'a region' or 'a community'. You're creating an individual's voice. That voice will be with the character through thick and thin, adapting accordingly. The following exercises help explore how the accent can behave when your character experiences high emotion, uses subtext and is in different physical states.

Accent and situation for actor
You will likely undertake accent work in various environments. You may be onstage, in a recording booth, in a studio or on location. You may have lots of time to prepare or very little. You may be playing one character or many, each with a different accent. The following exercises offer possible solutions to common issues and suggest ways of adapting both the accent and ways of working, so that you can flourish wherever you find yourself.

Accent and situation for character

Exercise: **Say the Subtext**

To help explore subtext and emotional range in accent
This exercise is often used in rehearsal rooms and acting classes but is less often used when engaging in more technical accent work. Find a scene or section of the text where there is subtext. Read it aloud in the accent.

Improvise an alternative version of the scene in which your character says exactly what they mean, rather than the words on the page. Let yourself run wild!

Reflect for a moment on how the accent felt and sounded. Read the scene again as written. By exploring what you don't say, you may find more variety in the accent when you come back to reading what you do say.

Exercise: **Situational Speech**

To explore variations in the character's accent

All humans, to a greater or lesser extent, modify the way they speak according to the situation they're in. Sometimes this is done consciously, sometimes unconsciously. Go through your piece and note down the different immediate settings the character is in.

Choose one setting, situation or set of circumstances to play with. Find a space and adapt it as much as you can to mirror the type of setting your character is in. For example, if they're in a restaurant, set up a table and chairs with plates, glasses and cutlery. Perhaps play some music in the background or the sound of people talking so you can talk over them.

Improvise a scene in the accent that takes place in this setting. It could be similar to a scene from the script or something different. You could speak to one character, several or even ones you've made up. Use your imagination to build the setting around you and notice what happens to the accent as you improvise.

If you have time, try improvising settings which don't appear in the piece. Here are some suggestions:

- a political rally
- babysitting a toddler
- training a dog
- a job interview
- working in customer service
- a sports event
- in their own bedroom

How did you sound in the different situations? Did the accent change and if so in what ways? Note down any discoveries.

Exercise: **Variation Station**

To improve confidence and flexibility in the accent
You need: an accent recording, some text

You might find this exercise helpful for gaining confidence, improving flexibility and lowering the stakes of text work in the accent.

Play the accent recording and listen out for a short phrase to copy in the accent. When you get to the phrase, pause the recording and copy it as closely as possible.

Copy the rhythm, stress, pitch and sounds of the phrase closely. Staying in the accent, say the same phrase in the following ways:

Happy	Fearful	Flirty
Sad	Disgusted	Confused
Angry	Surprised	Annoyed
Sleepy	Bored	Nauseous

Were you able to keep a sense of the accent as you changed the way you said the phrase? Don't worry if the accent went astray at times, this is just for practice.

Pick a line from your script. Say it out loud in the accent. Then do the same as you did before, using the list above to say the lines in different ways, while staying in the accent.

Exercise: **High Stakes Help**

To help maintain the accent in high stakes moments
You need: some text (optional)

The most common time an accent falters in performance is when the character is in a high stakes situation with high levels of emotion. It's often the point at which an actor reverts to their own habitual shape, patterns or sounds. This is understandable. High emotion and levels of tension are often embodied to such a degree that the character and actor become enmeshed for a moment. Unfortunately, it can also become the moment where the actor's own sounds are heard instead of the character's.

For very good reasons, actors often avoid over-rehearsing high stakes moments. However, avoiding exploring high emotion in an accent is a little like going onstage without choreographing a fight scene – you don't know where you will end up! One solution is to practise high stakes in the accent outside of your script, and to gradually build up to applying it to text.

Choose whether you would like to use an alternative script or improvise. Find a quiet space with room to move. You're going to experiment by taking the accent from a level 1 to a level 10 of emotion. The emotion you use is entirely your choice. It could be anger or fear but it could also be relief or excitement, for example.

Speak in the accent, starting at level 1. How do you address this emotion at this low level? Slowly build it up to 2, 3 and so on until you've reached level 10. Are you holding onto the sounds at each level or is there a point at which they start to slip? If so, move back down the scale to the level at which they were embedded and work up from there.

Try this with other emotions. Notice what happens to the accent. Do the sounds feel secure at every level? Did the rhythm and pitch change in line with the emotion?

When you have a sense of where the high stakes moments or lines are in the piece, use **Secret Sound**, **Accent Backstory** and/or **Target Practice**. These exercises can help you connect with why the character needs to use the sounds of their accent.

If you do practise high stakes moments on script and feel the accent slipping, try to isolate the word or sound it slips on. For example, the line could be 'I need you to go, now!' and you slip on the vowel in the word 'go'. Say the line in the accent without emotion, focusing on the sounds in 'go'. Say the line again, with more emotion. Notice any changes you've made to make the sound with your tongue, lips or jaw.

Find sounds and words around it which feel more stable. By switching the stress on these sounds and words or by relishing them, you can use them to anchor the accent in performance.

Exercise: **Under the Influence**

To help explore the accent of the character in an intoxicated state
Inspired by the work of Barbara Houseman
You need: some text
There may be part of the piece where your character's speech needs to be slurred because of intoxication from drugs or alcohol. Before you begin this exercise, it might help to find a recording of the accent where a speaker has been drinking, for example. Notice how the accent behaves when 'under the influence'.

Work in your own accent first. Read the first line of your text, sounding only the vowels, forget the consonants completely. Try to run smoothly from one vowel to the next, as if they were one long ribbon. You can put a tiny 'huh' at the beginning to help keep it smooth.

Do the same thing, but this time using the vowel sounds of the accent you're learning. If you would like to recap or refine the accent's vowels, the exercises **First Impression Vowels** (p. 142) and **Slow Motion** (p. 143) in Part B could be helpful. Read the text in the accent, adding the consonants back in very lightly to maintain the long ribbon of vowels. Does this help to sound intoxicated?

Accent and situation for actor

Exercise: **Create Your Shorthand**

To help get into the accent quickly for performance
Once you've learnt and prepared the accent thoroughly, it's helpful to gather ways of jump-starting it. This is especially helpful if you have limited warm-up time, long breaks between scenes or you're playing multiple roles.

- Think of one shape that helps you get into the accent. It could be 'round lips', or 'open jaw', or it could be a direction like, 'send the accent forward'. Take this on.
- Think of three key sounds of the accent. Make these three sounds through the shape of the accent.

- Say five words that feel easy to say in the accent. They could be from the script, made-up, local slang or even swear words. Whatever brings you the most confidence.
- Write a short sentence that contains these five words. Say this phrase a few times to get you ready for performance.

If you haven't tried **I Speak, Therefore I am** or **Secret Sound**, use them to explore the 'attitude' or 'personality' of the accent. Get into the shape of the accent and imagine yourself taking on the attitude.

Exercise: **Accent Warm Up**

To prepare for performing in the accent

It is worth creating your own accent warm-up to combine preparing your voice for performance with easing into the voice of the character using the features of the accent. Regardless of the accent, it's useful to release any excess tension you may be holding:

- Massage your shoulders and allow the breath to flow.
- Roll your shoulders forward and then back several times.
- Give your face a gentle massage. Explore the different parts: forehead, eyebrows, around the nose and the lips. Keep the breath flowing.
- Gently massage your jaw at the hinge. Think 'space' between the top and bottom teeth.
- Clean each tooth with the tip of your tongue and then massage under the chin.
- Blow raspberries through the lips.

Shapes

- Take on the shapes of the accent you've discovered. Breathe in and out through this posture.
- Hum and send the buzz to the resonant focal area you've found for the accent. Speak from this place.

Sounds

- Say each of the following phrases five times in the accent. Start slowly before increasing your speed:

Sarah and Rory cruised their barge under a narrow, red bridge.
Although Billy loved living in central Berlin, he literally longed for English trifle.
Think about this: does your brother Ethan breathe through his nose or his mouth?
Twenty-two little bottles sat out on the patio.

Text

- Take a chunk of text and speak it in the accent. Start slowly and gradually build up speed.
- Speak the same text focusing on your target.

Exercise: **Multi-Role Call**

To prepare for multi-role, multi-accent performances

If you're working on a multi-role performance where you're required to use different accents, it can be helpful to use **Create Your Shorthand** to get into each new accent quickly and easily. Make sure the phrases you write for each accent differ from one another.

Say these phrases one after the other in each accent. Focus your attention on the shifts in the shapes you make and enjoy the way your articulators move for each accent. Focus on the differences above all.

Closer to performance, treat the switchover as you would a fight call. Before you go onstage for each performance, find a quiet space or use the performance space if possible. Walk through and mark the shifts between characters, where you will have to change the accent.

Practise the end of the line in the first accent, and the beginning of the line in the second. Mark the shifts in shape and sounds.

Plan your offstage time between accents. Do you need to consult your shorthand to make a quick shift between accents, or do you have time to warm up into the new accent before you come back on? Build this work into your preparation.

Exercise: **Trippingly on the Tongue**

To help with intelligibility in the accent

Depending on the project, the medium or the needs of the moment, there may be occasions when you need to increase intelligibility in the accent.

Try to identify which moment, line or word needs work. It could already be clear to you, or you may have been directed to it. Experiment with the following tactics for increasing intelligibility:

Slow the pace of the line, or the key stress of the line. Say your line at a level 5 speed, bring it right down to level 1, and then try level 3. Don't forget to act – keep thought and intention in the line. Where did the balance of energy and intelligibility feel right to you?

Lengthen vowels. Pick a vowel in the line or word which you can afford to lean into for longer. Say the line and when you get to the vowel, imagine stretching it as if it were an elastic band. What effect did it have on the energy and thought behind the line?

Leave space around a word. Separating two or more words in a line can help increase intelligibility. Say the line and pick a word you feel needs to stand out from its neighbour. It could be the main stress of the line. Say the line again and leave a tiny break at the end of the word you chose, a slight 'suspension'. Repeat the line and this time, make the tiny break *before* you start the word. If this doesn't work for you, say the line and imagine there are inverted commas around the word you've chosen, for example I want to go to the 'shops' today. Reflect on the effect this had on the line.

Work the consonants. Speak the line and experiment with adding in a consonant sound which is regularly dropped in the accent (e.g. an H or a T sound). You could also make the release of one or two consonants in the line stronger, by adding voice or increasing the resistance to the airflow.

Exercise: **Changing Spaces**

To help prepare the accent for various performance spaces
You need: your text, recording device (optional)
Take a chunk of your text and speak it in the accent in as many different places as you can. These could include:

- an echoey space
- in front of a curtain
- into a glass or mug
- lying on the floor
- curling up on the sofa
- pushing against a wall
- as you walk
- over music
- outside

Notice what you found easier and more difficult and note down any surprises you encountered. Are there any spaces that require more consonant focus, for example, or a lengthening of vowels? If you're unsure, try recording yourself as you explore these different spaces and listen back. What do you need more or less of in that specific situation? Consider:

- articulation of vowels and consonants
- pace of speech
- space around or gaps between words
- volume
- resonant focus

Use the suggestions in **Trippingly on the Tongue** to help with clarity and audibility.

If you're touring a show, consider the different venues you may be performing in. Perhaps you'll be working on location in dry, dusty, hot weather, shooting a battle scene. The more work you've done on preparing the accent for the situation, the easier it will be to stay connected to the sounds in performance.

If you're wearing a costume, prosthetic, mask, headpiece or any other item of wardrobe or makeup which has the potential to affect your voice, it's worth looking at this as part of your accent preparation too. Find something that can imitate what you will be wearing and practise your lines using it.

Exercise: **Smudging Sounds**

To help blend sounds and words to find ease and credibility in the accent
You need: an accent recording of conversational, informal speech
Depending on the medium, the piece, the character and the moment, it may help to 'smudge' sounds to reshape the flow of the line and make it work for you. Think of yourself as an artist using charcoal, blurring and blending to add depth and detail to a picture.

Depending on what would be most helpful, appropriate and most importantly part of the accent, you might have the following options:

- Drop a sound
- Shorten a sound
- Exchange one sound for another
- Move the sound to a different part of the vocal tract
- Add voice to a sound
- Remove voice from a sound

There are even more combinations if you mix and match smudging options.

Listen to your accent recording and listen for any moments where the speaker 'smudges' the sounds along the lines of the previous list.

Use your discretion to 'smudge' sounds rather than altering anything significant in the writing. You may be in a professional situation where it's not appropriate to smudge parts of the text, for example in certain types of theatre or if production wants the lines exactly as written.

Part D   Troubleshooting

This part of the book outlines common issues with accent learning, along with solutions and directions to helpful exercises.

I feel as though I'm getting something wrong with the accent but I don't know what.

- What is it that you haven't thought about? Look at the Contents page, 'How to use this book' and the index. Try something you wouldn't normally do.
- Record yourself and listen back.
- Have you thought about **Shapes**?
- Have you considered the **Sounds**?
- Maybe you've bypassed **Patterns** of stress, rhythm or pitch?

A word sounds wrong, but I don't know why.

- It could be one or more of the sounds. Try **Consonant or Vowel**.
- If it's a consonant, use **Consonant Checklist** and go to the relevant consonant section.
- If it's a vowel, use **First Impression Vowels**, **The Long and the Short of It, Vowel Movements**, **Slow Motion** and **The Matisse**.
- It could be a particular vowel and consonant combination in a phrase. Try **Smudging Sounds** and/or **Trippingly on the Tongue.**
- It could be word stress. Try **Stress Ball**.

I'm having trouble with this one sound and can't work out why.

- Go to Part A: Speech to free yourself up.
- Be clear about which sound it is, using **Consonant or Vowel**.
- If it's a consonant, use **Consonant Checklist** and go to the relevant consonant section.

- If it's a vowel, use **First Impression Vowels**, **The Long and the Short of It**, **Vowel Movements**, **Slow Motion, The Matisse**.
- Build a relationship with it using: **Grit into Gold**, **Sound Personality**, **Tasting the Sounds**, **Accent Backstory**, **Secret Sound**.

How do I know if I'm doing it right?

- What is 'right'? What are your goals? Set a target so you know what you're aiming for.
- Listen to your accent recording and write a transcript of it. Record yourself replicating the accent recording word for word and sound for sound. Listen to the two recordings and compare them.
- Get feedback from someone you trust.
- Hire a coach if you can!

I am getting lost in the details and getting overwhelmed.

The following sections and exercises can help you loosen up and zoom out without losing track of the accent:

- Part A: Speech.
- **Have a Bash!**, **Free the Fear**, the 'Imitating' section.
- Patterns: **Verbatim Stress**, **Verbatim Rhythm**, **Verbatim Pitch**, **Ballroom Dancing**, **Playing the Pitch**.
- Sounds: **Vowel Song**, **Vowel Story**, **Moving the Story**, **Consonant Story**.

I'm short of time.

Prioritize. Here are some exercises to help:

- To find examples and get something out of them: **Search Party**, **First Impressions**.
- To find key features of the accent: the 'Discovering Shapes' section, **Which Way?**, **Move to the Music**, **Sound Shortlisting**, **Consonant Checklist**, **First Impression Vowels**.
- To practise key features of the accent: **Practise, Party! Practise, Party!**, **Colour Code**, **I Speak, Therefore I Am**, **Variation Station**.
- To get into the accent again quickly: **Accent Warm Up**, **Create Your Shorthand**.

I keep making the same mistakes and I'm feeling frustrated.

- Go back to basics. Become aware of your anatomy and your habits in Part A: Speech.
- Refocus using **Zen Master** or **Don't Fight the Fidget!**
- You may have just found some standout features using First Impression-type exercises. Explore those features in more detail using the exercises in Part B: Accent.
- Work on the few things you've prioritized as needing improvement using **Practise, Party! Practise, Party!**

I find it hard to improvise in the accent.

- Easy access = easy practice. Put your recording on a portable player, and make notes on your phone so you can look at them quickly whenever you need to.
- Use **Don't Fight the Fidget!** to get more familiar with the accent.
- Use exercises in the 'Shapes' and 'Resonant Focus' sections to find the overall sound quality of the accent.
- Use the following to build up a repertoire of sounds: **Vowel Story**, **Consonant Story**, **Slang Dictionary**, **Create Your Shorthand**.
- Use the following to become more familiar with the accent overall: **Stranger to Local**, **I Speak, Therefore I Am**, **Swear on Your Life**.

I enjoy improvising in the accent but struggle to take the accent into text.

- Use **Free the Fear**.
- Try any of the 'Accent and script' exercises in Part C: Acting.

Production wants text work before adding the accent, or the accent won't be decided on until later in the rehearsal/production process.

- If the accent has been decided on but you are not using it yet, start learning and improvise in it outside of rehearsals.
- Use the 'Listening' section, and/or **Stranger to Local**.
- Use the 'Patterns' and 'Shapes' sections in Part B: Accent.
- If the accent is decided on later, you may have less time to learn it. Use exercises that help prioritize and target your learning. See '**I'm short of time**' on p. 176 for suggestions.

I have an audition and the casting breakdown contains only minor details regarding accent. For example, it only says 'British'. What do I go for?

- Pick a specific example to work with. Use **Search Party** to help.

- Choose something that will work to your advantage. This could be something you've done before or something you are going to feel confident with in the audition.

I keep getting stuck in repetitive patterns.

- Try any of the following: **Once More With Feeling, Fascinating Rhythm, Unchained Melody, Intention Hunter, I Wish I'd Said That!, Say the Subtext, Situational Speech, Variation Station**.

Aspects of the accent feel at odds with my character.

- Try any of the following: **Make a Match, Secret Sound, Swear On Your Life, Say the Subtext**.

When I do the accent, it feels 'forced' or 'effortful'.

Narrow down what's wrong. Does it feel physically effortful, do you feel very 'conscious' of doing the accent, or is it a combination?

- Use Part A: Speech to loosen up.
- Use the 'Shapes' section to rediscover the articulator positions and movements for the accent.
- Take the accent away for a while and go back to the text using **Plot It**.
- Use **Scaffolding Sounds** to build up the accent in manageable chunks.
- Improvise in the accent using **The Interview, I Speak, Therefore I Am** and/or **Swear on Your Life**.

I don't know what to listen out for.

- Use the 'Listening' section, **First Impressions, Sound Shortlisting, Move to the Music, Draw the Patterns**.

I can't seem to hear or pick out individual sounds when listening.

- Slow the recording down if you can.
- Use **Zen Master** and **Don't Fight the Fidget** to find ease when listening.
- Use **First Impressions** to hone in on what stands out to you.
- Rather than listening for sounds, start by listening for interesting phrases or words.
- Use what you *can* hear: try the 'Shapes' or 'Patterns' section in Part B: Accent.
- Use **Consonant or Vowel** to explore the differences between sounds.

I'm worried about being 'offensive' or 'disrespectful' when learning this accent.

- Work in private, at least at first.
- Use **Have a Bash!** and/or **Free the Fear** to lower the stakes for yourself.
- Use the 'Listening' section and/or **Stranger to Local** to deepen your understanding of the accent and its background.
- Be thorough in your research and when practising so you can move past first impressions and avoid stereotyping.

I keep losing my way and going into another accent.

This may be happening because the accents share some features.

- Listen to examples of the two accents and explore what the key differences are. They could be sounds, patterns and/or shapes.
- Practise the key differences.
- Find your anchors: pinpoint where in a line or piece of text you wander and find a feature to root you and bring you back.

I can do the accent when concentrating on it but lose it when I'm in rehearsal or performing.

- Try any of the following: **High Stakes Help**, **Target Practice**, **Accent Backstory**, **Tasting the Sounds**.

I've been told the accent isn't 'clear' enough for the space I'm performing in.

- Use the 'Accent in situation' section, in particular **Trippingly on the Tongue** and **Changing Spaces**.

I've been told the accent needs to be 'light'. How do I achieve that?

- Use the 'Listening' section to help you define what you're looking for.
- Use **Search Party** to find an example.
- If you feel you can't hear the accent features clearly using your example, use a stronger example alongside it to compare features.

I can't find an accent recording which matches what I've been asked to do, for example I can't find the right age, social background or era.

- Use the 'Listening' section and **Search Party** to help.

- If you find a helpful real-life speaker, use **How to Generate Your Own Accent Recording** to make your own example.
- Work with what you *do* find. Even if it's not perfect, there may be some useful features in a recording. Use your judgement to find which parts of the accent recording would be suitable to copy for the project and character. Consider the patterns, shapes and sounds, using some of the exercises in Part B: Accent.

I've been asked to play a character with a mix of features from two different accents in their voice.

- Use **Search Party** to help you find a speaker with a similar mix of accents. Alternatively, find and explore examples of the two different accents.
- If possible, liaise with your project's creative team, bringing your own ideas and examples to the table.
- Seek the advice of a coach if you can.

I'm playing more than one role and need to change accents frequently and/or quickly.

- Try the **Multi-Role Call** exercise.

Appendix A: Accent recordings

Several accent recordings accompany this book **(https://www.bloomsburyonlin eresources.com/the-accent-handbook)**. These are accents that we're often asked to coach, as well as a variety of different accents from all over the world.

The accents included do not in any way have superiority over other accents. If we could have included every accent in the world, we would have!

Each accent is individual and unique and is by no means a representation of the whole town or city from which the speaker is from. Similarly, you may be from the place of a recording and may not recognize all the sounds as your own. That's because everyone has an **idiolect** (their own personal speech habits) and therefore may very well have key differences. Think of the recordings as examples of how someone from that place might speak, rather than how someone should speak.

If you can't find the accent you're looking for among the recordings provided, the 'Listening' section p. 33 can help you locate your own examples.

Appendix B: Recording material

Vowel sentences

KIT	This business is finished.
DRESS	Many eggs at breakfast.
TRAP	Snatch massive cans at the back.
LOT	Watch the stock pot.
STRUT	One punch drew a rush of blood.
FOOT	It could be put in a book.
BATH	Laughing staff asked to dance past.
CLOTH	The quarrel cost the officer.
NURSE	Search for the hurt girl in person.
FLEECE	Don't eat bees please.
FACE	Wait for a break to change.
PALM	His father calmly drank lager.
THOUGHT	Always caught drawing on the wall.
GOAT	Don't joke about the boat on the ocean.
GOAL	This bowl is old and mouldy.
GOOSE	You move balloons to a new room.
PRICE	I like to fight for my island.
CHOICE	Boys avoid noisy coins in oil.
MOUTH	A loud crowd on the roundabout.
NEAR	Here on the pier with a beer.
SQUARE	Hairless bears are scary.
START	My heart broke far apart.
NORTH	Laura ordered a wardrobe.
FORCE	Nora adores hoarding.
CURE	You're curiously pure on tour.
happY	Gerry was stupidly happy.
lettER	Doctor Foster mixed butter and sugar.
commA	Australia, America and Austria.
MARY	Merry Mary was to marry.
TRIOS	Noah the lawyer fired the player in an hour.

Consonant sentences

Sarah and Rory cruised their barge under a narrow, red bridge.
Although Billy loved living in central Berlin, he literally longed for English trifle.
Think about this: Does your brother Ethan breathe through his nose or his mouth?
The king was dancing and singing all night long.
Hamish and Hamoud hated having holidays in Hull.
Winston and Valentina wore high-visibility vests to West Virginia.
Twenty-two little bottles sat out on the patio.
Did you know the stupid duke ate tuna?
He knew the computer lured suitable cute newts.
It's a struggle to stroll down each street in this district.
The driver drove the train along tricky tracks drenched in droplets.
They gently cradled the little baby in the middle of the hospital.
The kitten had hidden buttons in the garden.
The thin velvety feather flew further with the help of a very healthy wind.
Do you think that turtles dance to smooth tunes or thumping beats?

Ghost Ship

This is not a ghost story. Or at least, I assume it isn't.

It was a raw and crisp Tuesday night in the middle of winter when I arrived at the shipyard. As I passed through the gates, it barely occurred to me that my first officer should have been there to greet me. I don't usually forget formalities, but this night was different. I was more interested in getting onboard and warming up.

Twenty-four hours ago, I'd been employed as Captain on a new ship called Sarah 2. The owner was a very wealthy businessman, Mr H, who had called me personally. Apparently, I was the only one for the job.

My journey was difficult. Delays due to thick fog had forced me to take a train through the mountains. The taxi driver at the station glanced in the rear-view mirror and refused to take me beyond the outskirts of the yard. Confused, I walked on past abandoned garages through a derelict scrubland area around the main fence.

The silence was strange. If it wasn't for the crunch of my footsteps on the ice, I might have questioned my own hearing. The visibility was poor, but I fought to see the dark outline of a ship at the end of a long wooden dock. I quickened my pace. My whole being was gripped with a desire to be met by somebody. Anybody.

As I stepped onto the jetty a strong gust of wind whipped past me. It whistled and screamed through the ships' masts. I was running now.

The dock shook as I thundered on. My eyes were fixed on a little light flashing in one of the boat's windows. More and more lights began to appear until it became a huge beacon. Someone must be on duty.

When I came to a stop, all I could hear was my own panting into the frozen air. As my breath began to calm, I tuned into the sound of a low hum inside the ship. The engines were running.

Now, this was odd. The boat wasn't in the water. She had been in this dry-dock for thirteen months. The glowing ship looked as if it was pure gold, but not a single person was there. I charged from room to room calling out for a solitary soul until my voice began to fail. Finally, I found the engine room and prized the door open with trembling fingers. The hum lured me down the metal steps, my palms clinging to the railings. Suddenly, a rasping scream made me whirl around in terror.

The last thing I saw as my eyes were clamped shut was something crawling towards me . . .

Conversation prompts

- Tell me about where you grew up.
- Tell me about your education.
- What is your fondest childhood memory?
- What is your favourite food and why?
- What makes you laugh out loud?
- Who do you text the most and why?
- What are the top three things on your bucket list?
- Who is the most influential person in your life?
- What would you do if you won the lottery?
- Do you think your priorities have changed over time?
- What was the most difficult thing you've ever done?
- What do people say about your accent?
- How does that make you feel?

Appendix C: Nonsense passage

Her extensive perceived may any sincerity extremity. Indeed add rather may pretty see. Old property delighted explained perceived otherwise objection saw ten her. Doubt merit the right these alone keeps. By sometimes intention smallness he northward. Consisted we otherwise arranging commanded discovery it explained. Does cold even song like two yet been. Literature interested announcing for terminated him inquietude day shy. Himself he fertile chicken perhaps waiting if highest no it. Continued promotion has consulted fat improving not way.

By so delight of showing neither believe he present. Deal sigh up in away when. Pursuit express no or prepare replied. Wholly formed old latter future but way she. Day her likewise smallest expenses judgement building man carriage. Considered introduced themselves to discretion at. Means among saw hopes for. Death mirth in oh learn he equal on.

Husbands ask repeated resolved but laughter debating. She end cordial visitor noisier fat subject general picture. Or if offering confined entrance no. Night rapturous him see something residence. Highly talked do so vulgar. Her use behaved spirits and natural attempt say feeling. Exquisite incommode immediate he something ourselves it of. Law conduct yet chiefly beloved examine village proceed.

Received shutters expenses he pleasant. Drift as blind above at up. No up simple county stairs do should praise as. Drawings together landlord had law smallest. Formerly welcomed attended declared met say unlocked. Just outlived no dwelling denoting in peculiar as he believed. Behaviour excellent be as it curiosity departure ourselves.

With my them if up many. Lay week nay she them her she. Extremity so attending objection as engrossed gentleman something. Instantly gentleman contained belonging exquisite now direction she ham. West room at sent if year. Numerous indulged distance old law you. Total state as merit court green decay he. Steepest bachelor the may delicate its yourself. As he instantly on discovery concluded to. Open draw far pure miss felt say yet few sigh.

Shot what able cold new the see hold. Friendly as an betrayed formerly he. Morning because as to society behaved moments. Put ladies design sister was. Play on hill felt john no gate. Am passed figure to marked in. Prosperous is inhabiting as assistance me especially. For looking two cousins regular among.

Possession her thoroughly remarkably terminated man continuing. Removed greater to do ability. You shy shall while but wrote marry. Call why sake has sing pure. So matter be me we wisdom should basket moment merely.

Appendix D: Vowel spelling guide

The following are examples of common spellings for each of the vowel groups. This can be helpful for pinpointing an accent's vowel sounds in text. They've been adapted from *Reference Vowels & Lexical Sets in Accent Acquisition* by Douglas N. Honorof.[1]

KIT
Typical: i (ship)
Other: y (myth), e (pretty), ui (guilt), o (women), ie (sieve), u (busy)

DRESS
Typical: e (step), ea (deaf)
Other: a (any), ie (friend), ai (said), ei (Leicester), u (bury)

TRAP
Typical: a (cat)
Other: ai (plaid).

LOT
Typical: o (stop)
[op, ot, ock, otch, oth, ob, odd, og, odge, om, on, oll, olve, omp, ont, opse, ox, off, oss, ov]
Other: a (watch), ow (knowledge)

STRUT
Typical: u (cup), o (done)
Other: ou (touch), oo (blood)

FOOT
Typical: u (put), oo (good), ou (could),
Other: o (woman)

BATH
Typical: aff (staff), ath (path), ass (class), aft (raft), asp (grasp), ast (fast), ask (mask), augh (laugh)
Other: ance (chance), ant (grant), anch (ranch), ample (example), alf (half), alv (halve), an't (can't), ana (banana), ans (answer) and (demand),

Unpredictable (BATH/TRAP):

corral, morale, graph/graphic, masque/masquerade, pastoral, exasperate, circumstantial, intransigent, substantial, transit, transport, transfer, transform, transitory, transient, transept, and other words in trans-; contralto, alto, plaque, Cleopatra.

CLOTH

Typical: o (gone), ou (cough), au (sausage)

Other: a (wash), or (origin), aur (laurel), ar (warrant)

NURSE

Typical: ur (hurt), or (work), ir (bird), er (term), ear (earth)

Other: yr (myrtle), our (journal), eur (connoisseur)

FLEECE

Typical: ee (meet), e (these), ie (brief), ei (ceiling)

Other: ea (meat), eo (people), oe (phoenix), ae (Caesar), ua (quay), i (ski)

FACE

Typical: a (tape) ai (wait), ay (play), ey (they), ei (rein), eigh (weigh),

Other: ea (great), au (gauge)

PALM

Typical: al (calm), -a (ma), ah (blah)

baht, Bach, facade, couvade, roulade, raj, taj, salaam, Brahms, Kahn, Afrikaans, kraal, Transvaal, Taj Mahal, spa, Shah, Pooh-Bah, Armagh, schwa, cantata, inamorato, legato, sonata, staccato, pizzicato, Lusaka, Karachi, mafia, 2 Dada, bravado, incommunicado, Mahdi, Mikado, laager, lager, Zhivago, (maha)rajah, kava, guava, Java, Swazi, Dali, Mali, Guatemala, Somali(a), lama, llama, Yokohama, swami, Brahmin, guano, piano ('softly'), marijuana, iguana, Botswana, (maha)rani, ha-ha, Malawi, Bahai, Sumatra, candelabra.

PALM/BATH

Typical: boa, bah, Koran, khan, Pakistan, Shan, chorale, rationale, locale, khaki, pasha, Nazi, Colorado, enchilada, Nevada, aubade, lava, palaver, plaza, almond, drama, pajama/pyjama, panorama, Ghana, nirvana, sultana, soprano, piranha, Bali, finale.

THOUGHT

Typical: augh (caught), ough (fought), au (cause), aw (crawl), al (salt), all (fall), alk (walk)

Other: a (water), oa (broad)

GOAT

Typical: oa (road), o (both), oe (toe), ou (soul)

Other: ow (own), ough (dough), ew (sew), au (gauche), oo (brooch), eau (beau)

GOAL

Typical: ol (old, roll), oal (coal), oul (mould), owl (bowl)

GOOSE

Typical: oo (tooth), o (who, move), ou (you, through)
Other: u (rude), eu (feud), ew (few), ui (juice), iew (view), eaut (beauty)

PRICE

Typical: i (side), y (type, dye), ig (fight, sign), ei (height),
Other: ai (aisle), oi (choir), uy (buy)

CHOICE

Typical: oi (join)
Other: oy (toy, buoy)

MOUTH

Typical: ou (house), ow (down)
Other: ough (plough), eo (MacLeod)

NEAR

Typical: ear (fear), eer (beer, eerie), ere (here), ier (pier, fierce), er (hero)
Other: eir (weird)

SQUARE

Typical: -are (care), -air (pair, fairy), ear (wear), -eir (their), -ere (there), ary (vary)
Other: ar (scarce), aer (aerial)

START

Typical: -ar (bar), ar (scarf, safari), ear (heart)

NORTH

Typical: or (for, sort), ar (war, warp)
[ort, orpe, ork, orque, orch, orch, orph, orse, ors, orb, ord, orge, orm, orn, orpse, orp, orf, orth, org, orw]
Other: uar (quarter), aur (aura, Laura)

FORCE

Typical: -ore (before), -oar (soar), -oor (door), -our (four),
Other: or- (port, pork, porch, divorce, afford, forge, torn, portrait, proportion, Borneo, oral, porous, story, Tory, glorious, historian, memorial)
oar- (board), our- (source, mourn)

CURE

Typical: oor (poor), our (tour),
Other: ure (sure), ur (curious), eur (Europe)

happY
Typical: -y (ready), -i (taxi), -ie (movie)
Other: -ee (coffee), -ey (money), -ea (Chelsea)

lettER
Typical: -er (butter) -re (metre), -ar (sugar) -or (major) , -o(u)r flav(o)ur, -yr (martyr), -ure
(pleasure)

commA
Typical: -a (visa, saga), -ia (dementia)

Notes

Introduction

1 J. Harrington, S. Palethorpe, and C. Watson, 'Does the Queen Speak the Queen's English?', *Nature* 408 (2000): 927–8, https://doi.org/10.1038/35050160 (accessed 20 April 2022).
2 The Off Camera Show, 'Willem Dafoe: Abandon Perfection, Try to Fail', Posted 9 April 2020, https://www.youtube.com/watch?v=1dSRzxg7p1E (accessed 21 January 2023).

Imitating

1 R. Oades, 'What Is Headphone-Verbatim Theatre?', https://www.roslynoades.com/about (accessed 1 November 2022).

Accent and character

1 T. Wenn, 'The Surprising Benefits of Swearing', *BBC Future*, 3 March 2016, https://www.bbc.com/future/article/20160303-the-surprising-benefits-of-swearing (accessed 1 September 2023).

Appendix D

1 J. C. Wells, 'Lexical Sets, from J.C. Wells', *Accents of English: Introduction* Chapter 2. Typical spellings taken from *Reference Vowels & Lexical Sets in Accent Acquisition* by Douglas N. Honorof, https://www.yorku.ca/earmstro/courses/phonetics/lexical_sets.pdf (accessed 2 May 2023).

Bibliography

Caban, Andrea, Julie Foh, and Jeffrey Parker, *Experiencing Speech: A Skills-Based, Panlingual Approach to Actor Training*, New York and London: Routledge, 2021.

Carey, David and Rebecca Clark Carey, *The Verbal Arts Workbook*, London: Methuen Drama, 2010.

Hagen, Uta with Haskel Frankel, *Respect for Acting*, New York: Wiley Publishing, Inc., 1973.

Hayden Rowles, Jan and Edda Sharpe, *How to Do Accents*, London: Oberon Books, 2007.

Honorof, Douglas N., 'Reference Vowels & Lexical Sets in Accent Acquisition', *Voice and Speech Review* 3, no. 1 (2003): 106–22, https://doi.org/10.1080/23268263.2003.10739387 (accessed 1 November 2022).

Houseman, Barbara, *Finding Your Voice: A Step-by-Step Guide for Actors*, London: Nick Hern Books, 2002.

Knight, Dudley, *Speaking with Skill: An Introduction to Knight-Thompson Speechwork*, New York and London: Bloomsbury, 2012.

Leveroy, Deborah, 'A Date with the Script: Exploring the Learning Strategies of Actors Who Are Dyslexic', *Theatre, Dance and Performance Training* 6, no. 3 (2015): 307–22, https://doi.org/10.1080/19443927.2015.1065464 (accessed 1 November 2022).

Linklater, Kristen, *Freeing the Natural Voice*, London: Nick Hern Books, 2006.

Wells, J. C., *Accents of English: Volume 1*, Cambridge: Cambridge University Press, 1982.

Index